Getting Ready to READ
Readiness Fundamentals

What is Readiness for Learning?

Children need to have developed competence in many areas before they begin the higher level learning skills of reading, math, etc. Some of these areas children have to "grow" into; for example, writing requires small muscle maturation. Others are developed through experience. The activities in *this book* will help children develop their social, motor, listening, visual perception, and oral language skills.

There is no clear-cut boundary between the various skills listed below. There is much over-lapping. For instance, if you are playing "Did You Ever See a Lassie?", students will be using their listening and visual discrimination skills to hear and see what to do and using their motor skills to do the movement. For convenience sake, these multi-skill activities are placed in only one of the category designations.

No one skill takes precedence over the others. They are all important. The developmental level of your students will determine how much of each section you do before moving on to the next skill. Be prepared to move back and forth through the categories as your students develop both in maturity and knowledge.

★ ★ Table of Contents ★ ★

Congratulations on your purchase of some of the finest teaching materials in the world.

Author: Jo Ellen Moore
Editor: Bob DeWeese
Illustrator: Joy Evans
　　　　　 Jo Supancich
Production Asst: Michelle Tapola

Entire contents copyright ©1995 by EVAN-MOOR CORP.
18 Lower Ragsdale Drive, Monterey, CA 93940-5746

Social Skills

Children arrive in our classrooms with varying degrees of social development. Whether confident or shy, adept at social situations or filled with problems, they appear on our doorsteps ready to become a part of the classroom "family" we work together to create.

The classroom at any grade level needs to be a place where children can learn as much as possible in a safe and caring environment; a place where children learn to respect themselves and to respect the rights of others. This is especially important with our very young students.

Provide a positive example for your students by modeling good manners, showing consideration of others, expressing your feelings, and admitting your mistakes.

Be generous with praise and stingy with criticism. Point out positive actions as they happen in the classroom and on the playground. Tell the class what you observe. Tell parents the positive actions you see.

Celebrate individual and class successes.

Provide experiences that help children,
in age appropriate ways, to:

- share materials and toys
- share the attention of the teacher and other adults
- take turns
- be responsible
- cooperate
- solve problems
- begin to understand their own feelings
- be aware of and sensitive to other people
- begin to experience collaborative play

       Readiness Fundamentals

Developing Self-Esteem

We want to help our children reach a true feeling of self-esteem; to have a strong belief in themselves. This is necessary for successful learning. This is necessary for a happy life.

• Children need to feel safe
No one can learn in an atmosphere of fear. Children need to know that the classroom is a safe place for them to be physically, and a safe place for them take risks in learning new skills and ideas.

• Children need to be treated with respect
We all need to be treated with respect if we are going to learn to treat others with respect. This includes being aware of individual rates of development and learning. Children need support at each level of success and failure.

• Children need to learn limits
Without a structure and understandable limits, children often have a feeling of being out of control. Limits help create less confusion in their lives by providing clear guidelines from which to operate their lives.

• Children need to receive support
They need a lot of nurturing and support as they tackle new skills and develop strategies for coping with their lives.

• Children need develop good communication skills
Being able to let others know how they are feeling and what they are saying, empowers children in an often confusing world. This also includes helping children understand how others are feeling and what they saying. They need to grow in the understanding that communication is a two-way street.

• Children need to be challenged
Appropriate challenges on a regular basis help children expand their levels of competence as they attempt, and in time master, new skills. These challenges must be carefully planned. They need to be motivating, without causing undo frustration. They need to encouraging, not discouraging.

• Children need to learn effective ways to deal with problems
They need to feel in control of themselves and their surroundings. This does not mean controlling others. It means learning to take care of themselves as much as they are able. It means solving their own problems as much as they can without always relying on the help of others, especially adults.

• Children need to have their talents and intelligence nurtured
There are many types of intelligences among any group of children. These need to be supported and given the opportunity to grow without one type being valued over the others. Our future teachers, artists, government leaders, humanitarians, etc. are in our classrooms right now.

Classroom Environment

We are the Children of America

Part of our goal to help children have a strong sense of self-esteem as well as an acceptance of others can be met by making sure the classroom reflects all of the cultures and ethnic groups represented in our country. This should be reflected in the pictures on display, in the books you read, etc. This bulletin board is an excellent beginning.

Display a photograph and information about each child in your classroom using the caption "We are the Children of America." Younger children will need to dictate information about themselves. Children who are writing can create anything from one paragraph to a full-fledged autobiography to accompany his/her photograph.

Have children trace their own hands then cut several copies out of different colors of construction paper. (If you have access to construction paper in many skin tones use this for the hand cut-outs.) Frame the bulletin board with these hands.

This is My Place!

Provide an area where each child can have a "bulletin board" of his/her own. Staple a large sheet of construction paper per child at a level the child can easily see. (Older students may be responsible enough to pin their own items on the board using large push pins. Younger students will need an adult to do this part.)

The child becomes responsible for deciding what goes in the space and how often it is changed. It becomes a spot for work the child is proud of, a special painting, or something from home he/she wants to share with the class.

Getting to Know You

★ **Around the Friendship Circle**

Have children sit in a circle. Give one child a beanbag. He/She tosses the beanbag to someone else in the circle. That person ask a question he/she would like to know about the other children in the room. Beginning on that person's left, go around the circle giving each child a chance to answer the question. Allow "I pass." to be an acceptable answer, as some children may not want to answer some questions. When everyone has had a chance to answer, the person holding the beanbag tosses it to someone else in the circle. That person asks the next question and you proceed as before.

★ **Friends Help Each Other Do a GREAT Job**

Take photographs of your students working together. Display these photographs with the good work they produce.

★ **Class Scrapbook**

Begin a class scrapbook the first day of school. This is a place for photographs of the children on field trips and in action at school. It is a place to put samples of projects created by the class. It is a place to record special events (lost teeth, new pets, new babies at home, visitors to class, etc.). Place the scrapbook in a place where children can go through it often; to remember the events happening as the year passes.

Class Rules

You and your students need certain behaviors in order to have a safe, happy environment where maximum learning can take place. The rules and consequences necessary to achieve this type of environment will vary from class to class and are greatly affected by the age and maturity of the children.

- **Keep any rules to a minimum.**
- **State them clearly.**
- **Be consistent.**

Consequences must be fair, reasonable, and age appropriate. You are not aiming for "punishment," only to help children understand that their actions have consequences and to maintain a positive classroom environment.

It is important to involve parents in this process. Keep them informed of what your expectations are and how they can be of help. Always keep in mind that they have known this child longer than you. Take advantage of that knowledge. Send letters home explaining class behavior expectations and consequences. Invite them to visit the class whenever possible; make them feel an important part of the classroom community.

Words Can Help or Hurt

Words that Help

Discuss words and phrases that help us get along with one another.

Role play situations that require the use of these words. Have two or three children act out a scene where they use these words. For example, have one or two children playing with the blocks. Another child walks up and ask, "May I play with the blocks with you?" Or have one child walk in between two others saying "Excuse me." as he/she passes.

I'm sorry...

- thank you
- excuse me
- may I help you
- may I play with you
- please
- I'm sorry
- I won't do it again

Words that Hurt

Discuss what teasing and name-calling is. Talk about how it makes people feel, and, to the best of your students' abilities, how to stop it.

Teach them this little verse.

Teasing isn't funny

Let me tell you why.

Teasing isn't funny

'Cause it makes people cry.

 # Feelings

How do they feel?
Cut a collection of faces from magazines. Use these for one or more of the following activities.

1. Show the pictures one at a time and have children describe how they think the person feels.

2. Show one picture. Say "This person feels happy." "What makes YOU feel happy?" Continue with other feelings.

3. Have a group of children sort the pictures into categories.

4. Put up large sheets of butcher paper. Label each sheet with a feeling word. Pass out your set of magazine pictures. Have children decide on which chart the picture belongs and paste it there.

Feeling Cards
Reproduce the cards on page 11. Give each child two or more of the cards (happy, sad, frightened, angry). Describe a situation appropriate to the age of your students. Have children show you the card that expresses how they would feel in that situation. Discuss differences in reactions.

Tonya feel down and skinned her knee.
Carlos won a bicycle in a contest.
Larry dropped his ice cream cone on the street. A dog came along and licked it up.
Maggie had a bad dream that woke her up. She couldn't go back to sleep.
Michael's best friend gets to spend the night at his house.
Kim couldn't find her mother in the store.

My Feelings are O.K.
Reassure children that everyone has feelings of many kinds and that this is the way it should be.

Teach this verse.

Each day as I'm growing
I'm glad to be knowing
These feelings
I feel
Are O.K.

Feeling Cards

 Readiness Fundamentals

Cooperation

Discuss how some things we can and should do by ourselves, while others work best when we do them together. Ask children to tell you something they can do by themselves. When everyone has had a turn, ask them to tell you something they do with at least one other person.

Describe a situation. Have children decide if it is something that can be done alone or something that needs cooperation. (Accept any reasonable answer.)

take a nap   get a drink of water
jump rope   paint a picture
move a table   clean up the classroom
eat lunch   play a game

Have children paint pictures of themselves doing with someone else. Post these on a bulletin board with a sign saying "Working and Playing Together."

Teach them this verse.

I help you.

You help me.

It's very simple,

Can't you see?

Cooperation

Get's the job done.

Cooperation

Makes the work fun.

Readiness Fundamentals

Responsibility

I Can Help (Myself, My Family, My World)
Discuss the ways children help at home and school.

At home I...
- pick up my toys when I'm done
- brush my teeth without being told
- don't slam the door when I go in and out
- play with my baby sister while mommy cooks dinner

At school I...
- keep my area clean
- put things away when I am done
- listen when the teacher is talking
- help take care of the class pets
- water the plants when it is my turn
- wash my hands before snack time
- hang up my sweater/coat

In my neighborhood I...
- throw my trash in the trash can
- put cans in the recycle bin
- am careful when I play

 Readiness Fundamentals

You Can Count on Me

If your students are mature enough, discuss topics such as these:

 Truth

If we want people to trust us, they need to believe us when we tell them the truth. Sometimes this is scary to do.

 Obedience

Who should we obey? When? Why? Should we always obey those who are older than us/adults?

 Rules

Why do we have rules? Who makes the rules? What happens when we break rules?

 Dependability/Responsibility

We do what we say we will do. We finish our jobs. We take care of our belongings. We help at home, at school, and in our world.

 Choices

Sometimes we make good choices; sometimes we make poor choices.

Readiness Fundamentals

Start with a Story

Libraries are full of wonderful books for children that help them explore feelings and share the experience of growing up. Use stories, fairy tales, and poems that incorporate conflict, raise value issues, and help students reach out to others and to the past. Select those appropriate for your students. Here are some examples to help you get started.

Some of the older books on this list are out of print. They are worth the effort of checking your school or public library shelves.

Goldilocks and the Three Bears (your favorite) -
  responsibility; honesty; consequences
The Friend by John Burningham (1976, Crowell)
  being friends isn't always easy
Arthur's Chicken Pox by Marc Brown (1994, Little)
  illness; jealousy
Grandmother and I by Helen Buckley (1994, Lothrop)
  fear; being comforted
Mama, Coming and Going by Judith Caseley (1994, Greenwillow)
  new baby in the house
It Takes a Village by Jane Cowen-Fletcher (Scholastic)
  responsibility; cooperation
Tough Boris by Mem Fox (1994, Harcourt)
  grieving over death of a pet
The Great Big Scary Dog by Libby Gleeson (1994, Tambourine)
  fear; problem solving
My bike by Donna Jakob (1994, Hyperion)
  learning a new skill
Beginnings: How Families Come to Be by Virginia Kroll (1994, Whitman)
  different kinds of families - traditional, adopted, single parents, etc.
All by Myself by Anna Grossnickle Hines (1984, Clarion)
  responsibility
Molly Lies by Kay Chorao (1979, Seabury Press)
  telling lies; consequences
Move Over Twerp by Martha Alexander (1981, Dial)
  problem solving
Sam by Ann Herbert Scott (1967, McGraw-Hill)
  loneliness; feeling left-out
When You Were a Baby by Ann Jonas (1982, Greenwillow)
  responsibility; growing up

Look at Us!

Mirror Image
You will need several hand mirrors for this activity.
1. Each child looks in the mirror and describes his/herself to the group.
2. Each child looks into the mirror and draws his/herself. Provide skin colored crayons for this activity.

Paint Center
Have children paint themselves and their classmates. Mix all shades of skin colors and hair colors for children to use. Have a place to display the finished paintings.

Alike and Different
Incorporate activities into your daily lessons to help students develop a positive view of themselves and others.

1. How are we alike?
Discuss the things that are the same about all people. Keep this on a very simple level; we all eat, we like to play, we sleep, etc.

2. How are we different?
Discuss the physical ways we are different; size, sex, hair color, skin color. Discuss the cultural differences; differences in languages we speak, things we eat, holidays we celebrate, etc.

3. What is special about (name student)?
Give children an opportunity to share what they see as special about their classmates. "Sam makes me laugh." "Maggie gave me half of her cookie." "Leroy always takes turns."

 Readiness Fundamentals

Track Progress, Reward Success

The reproducible materials on pages 18 through 32 can be used to help children see, in concrete ways, that they are being successful. Use the awards, mobiles, puzzles, and headband to award improvement and risk-taking as much as academic learnings and good behavior.

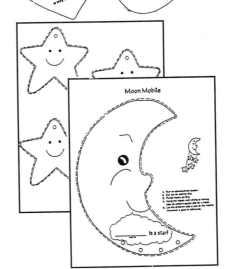

Awards
Page 18, 19, 27
Use these pages to track and reward student work and behavior.

Mobiles
Pages 20-23
Reproduce the rocket ship and space creatures. Cut the pieces out and glue to heavy paper (or have the child do this). Add a space creature with a piece of string or yarn each time the child reaches a goal or shows an understanding of a new skill or concept. Hang the mobiles around the classroom, then send them home when a child has earned all of his/her space creatures. Follow the same directions for the moon and stars mobile.

Headbands
Page 24-26
Reproduce the headbands on colored paper if possible. Cut out the pieces (or have the child do this step) and paste the band to fit the child's head. Use headbands to reward success in any area or give for special occasions such as birthdays.

Puzzles
Page 28-31
Reproduce the puzzle forms. Place the page containing boxes on a piece of colored paper and tape it to the child's desk. Cut the puzzle pieces apart and keep in an envelope marked with the child's name. Each time the child reaches a goal you have set for him/her, give one piece of the puzzle. The child pastes the piece in the correct box on his/her paper. The completed puzzle shows a picture (six part monkey or nine part bear). The completed puzzle is then sent home with a note to parent explaining the child's success.

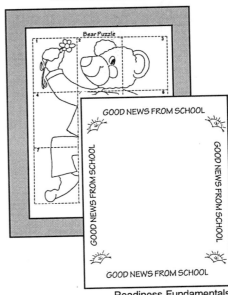

Stationary Form
Page 32
Keep parents informed about an individual child by reproducing the form and using it as stationary. The form can also serve as a newsletter to all parents. Simple write your message on the form, then reproduce as many copies as you need.

Readiness Fundamentals

Note: Reproduce these hearts to reward acts of kindness.

Kind Heart Awards

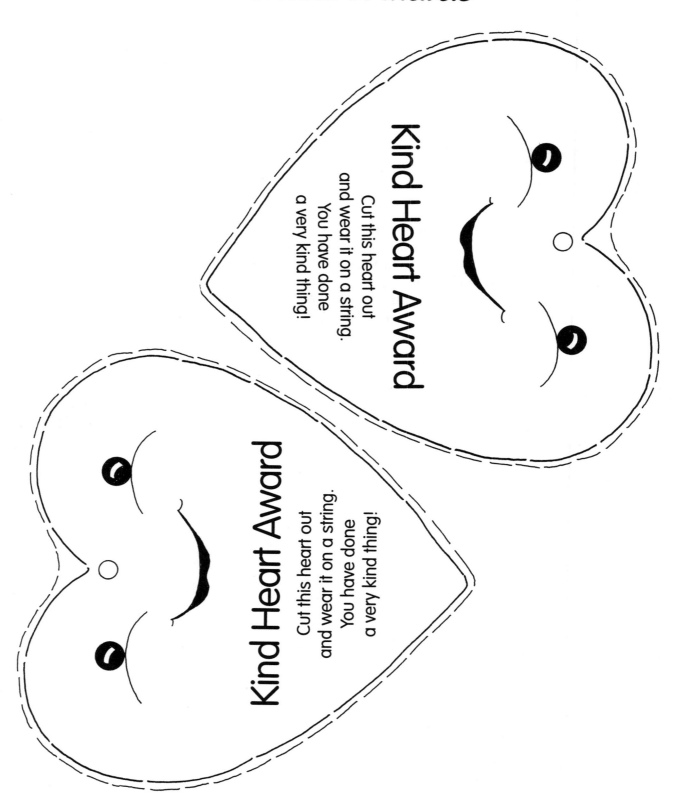

Kind Heart Award

Cut this heart out
and wear it on a string.
You have done
a very kind thing!

Kind Heart Award

Cut this heart out
and wear it on a string.
You have done
a very kind thing!

Note: Reproduce these hands to reward cooperation and helpfulness.

Helping Hand Award

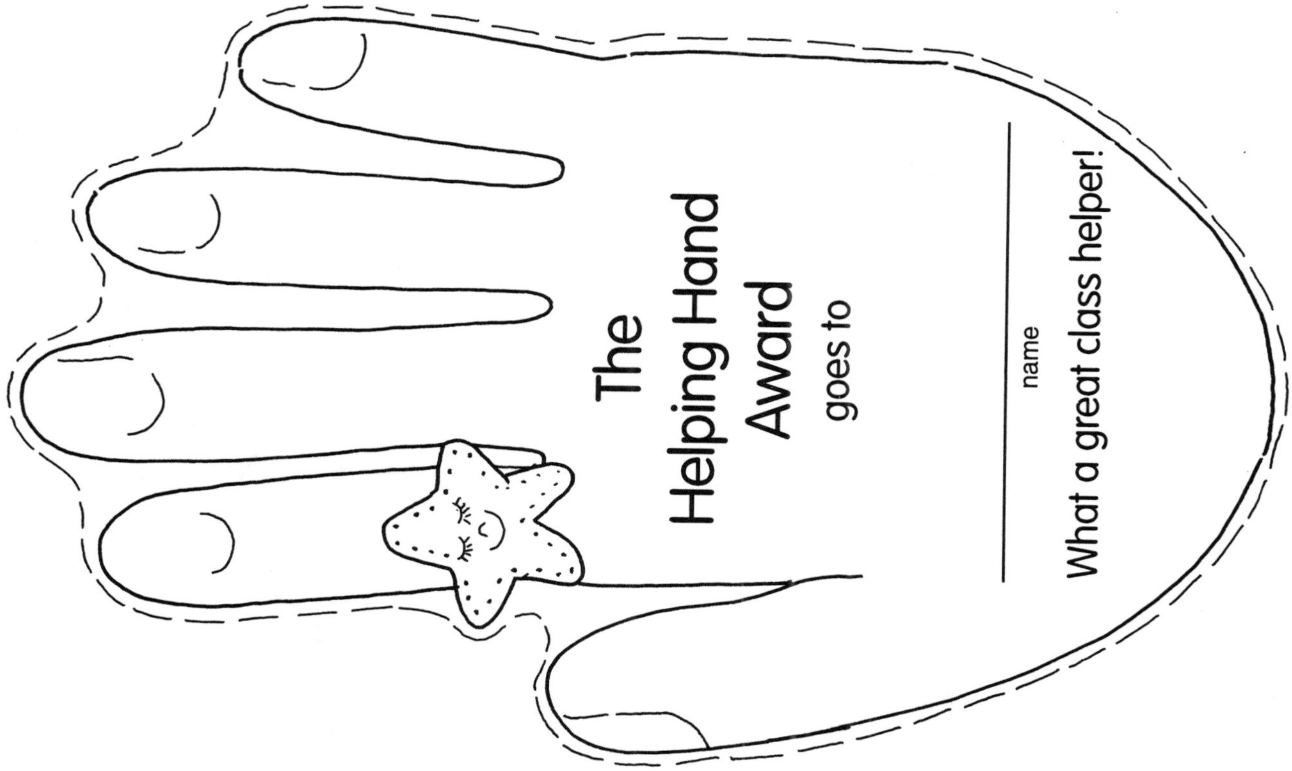

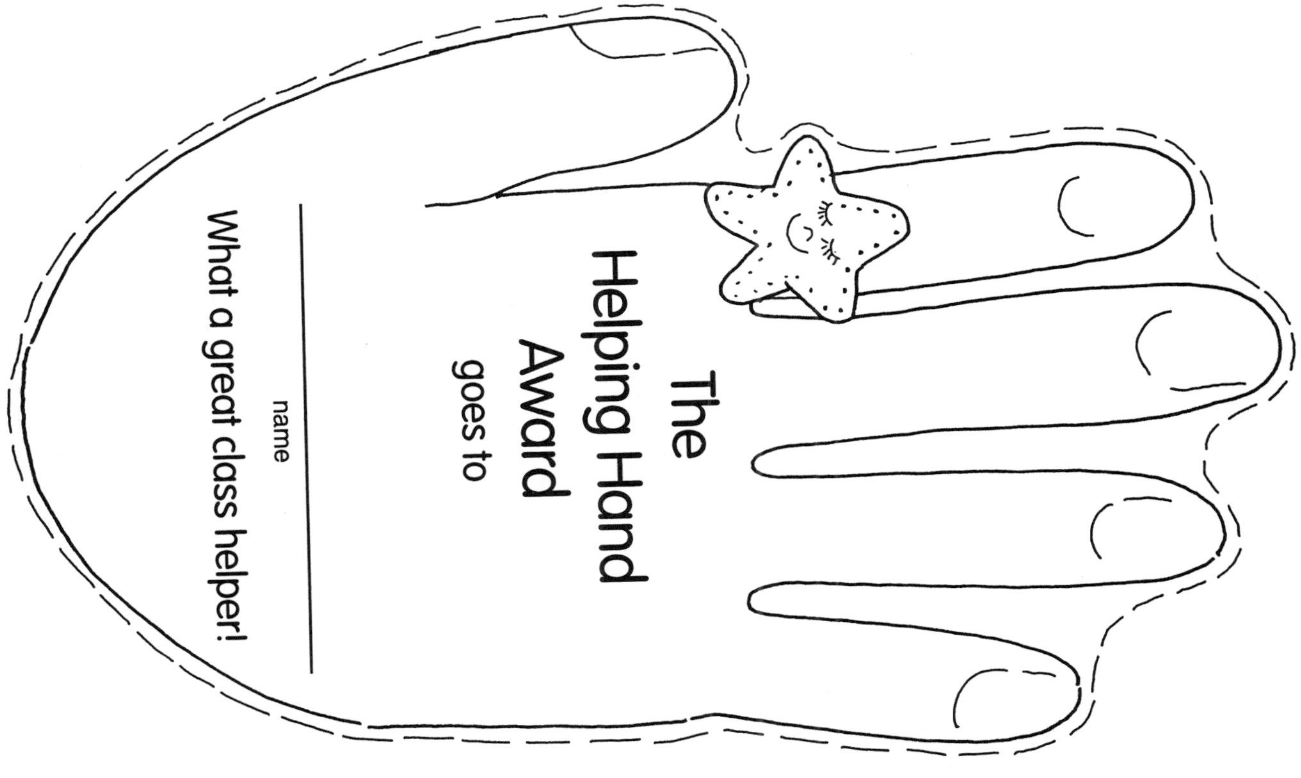

The
Helping Hand
Award
goes to

_____
name

What a great class helper!

The
Helping Hand
Award
goes to

_____
name

What a great class helper!

Note: Reproduce this mobile to reward children reaching preset goals.

Rocket Reward Mobile

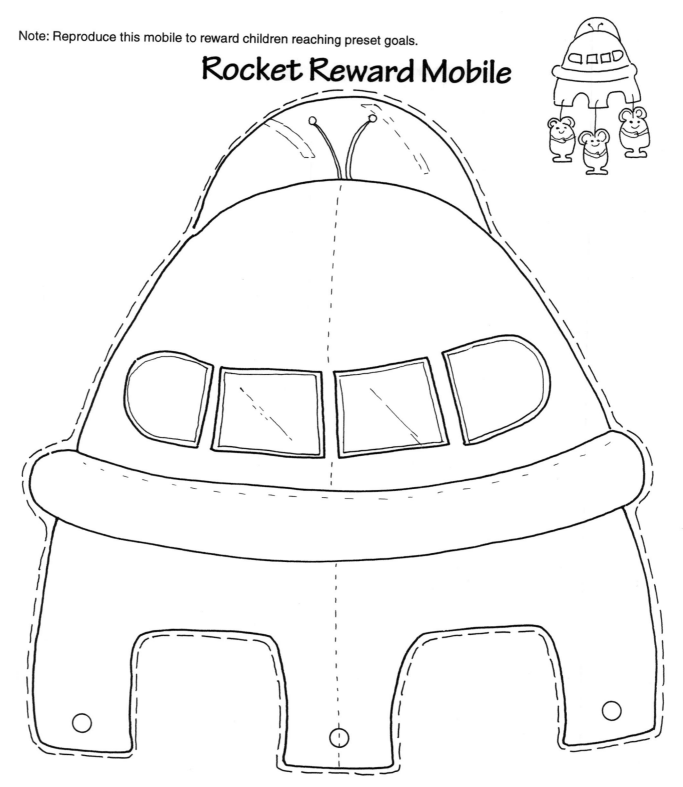

1. Run on construction paper.
2. Cut out on dotted line.
3. Punch holes on O's.
4. Hang the rocket with string or roving.
   Use an unbent paper clip for a hook.
5. Let the children add a Martian Man
   to the mobile whenever a goal is achieved.

20   Readiness Fundamentals

Note: Use these space creatures to complete the mobile on page 20.

Readiness Fundamentals

Note: Reproduce this mobile to reward children reaching preset goals.

Moon Mobile

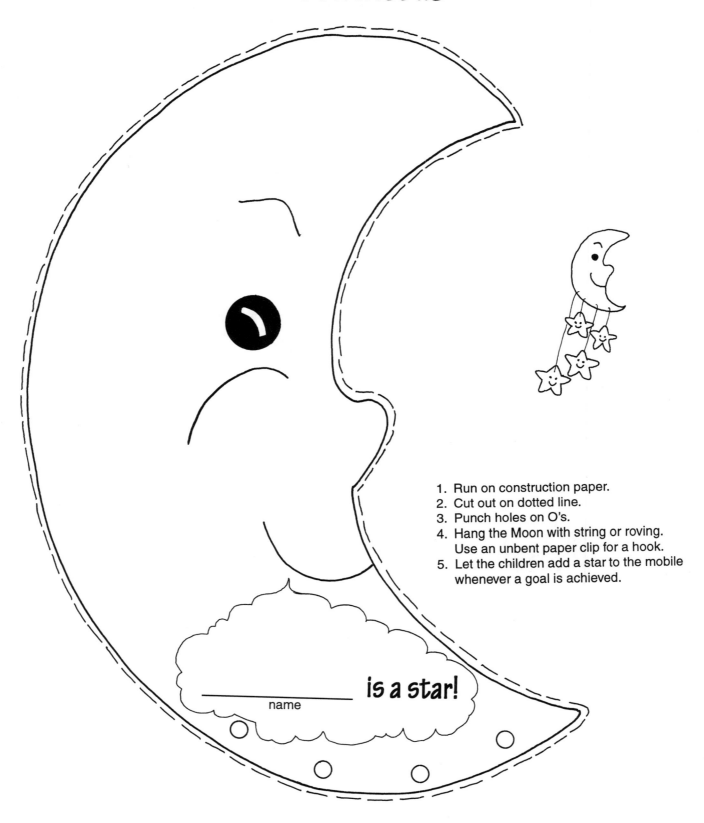

1. Run on construction paper.
2. Cut out on dotted line.
3. Punch holes on O's.
4. Hang the Moon with string or roving. Use an unbent paper clip for a hook.
5. Let the children add a star to the mobile whenever a goal is achieved.

_____ is a star!
name

Readiness Fundamentals

Note: Reproduce these stars to complete the mobile on page 22.

paste

1. **Color**
2. **Cut**
3. **Paste**
4. **Wear me home.**

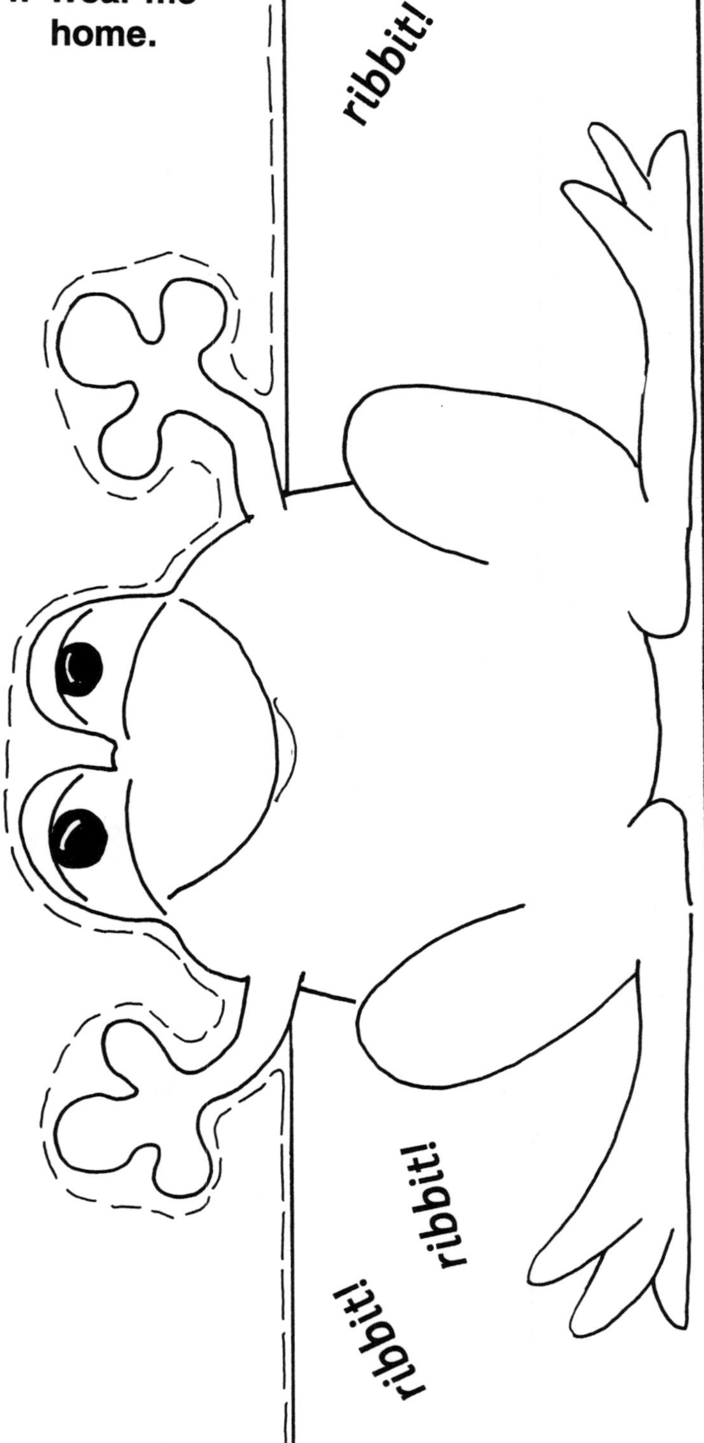

ribbit!

Ribbit! Ribbit! I did it! I did it!

ribbit!

ribbit!

paste

Note: Reproduce this headband to track what the student knows about himself/herself.

paste

1. **Color**
2. **Cut**
3. **Paste**
4. **Wear me home.**

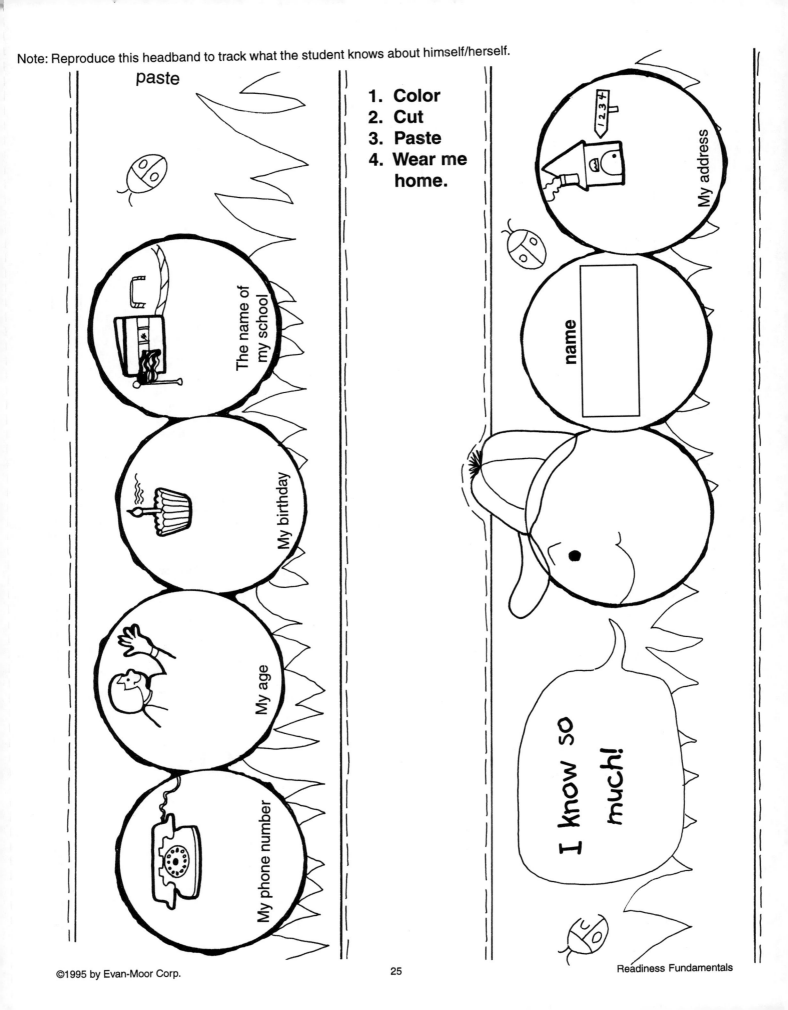

The name of my school

My birthday

My age

My phone number

My address

name

I know so much!

25

Readiness Fundamentals

Note: Reproduce this headband to reward success or to give out on special occasions such as a birthday.

1. **Color**
2. **Cut**
3. **Paste**
4. **Wear me home.**

paste

Super Star

paste

26

Readiness Fundamentals

_____

_ _ _ _ _ _ _ _ _ _ _ _ _ _

_____
Name

Every red apple on this tree,
Means a job well done
by me!

27

Readiness Fundamentals

Note: The child receives one puzzle piece each time a goal is reached.

Monkey Puzzle

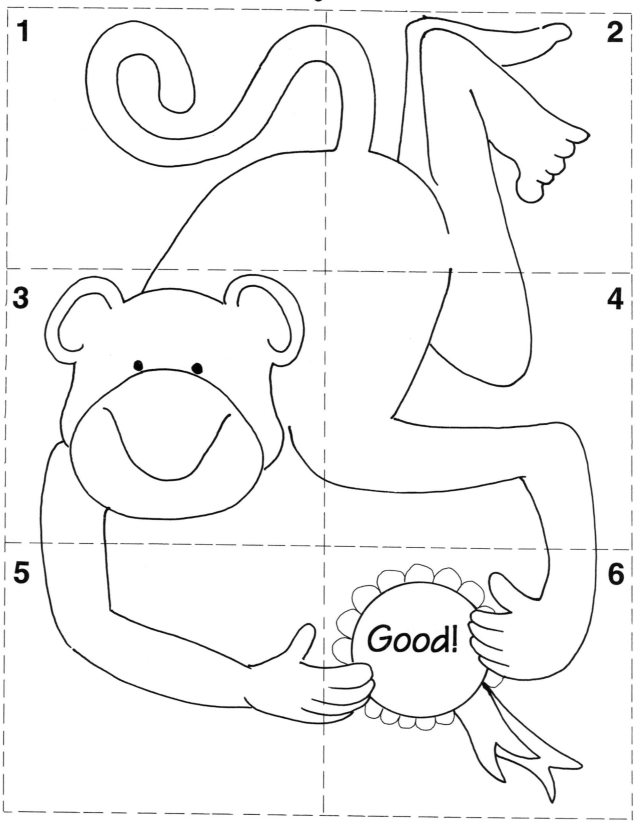

Mystery Puzzle

Paste puzzle here. Match the numbers.

1	**2**
3	**4**
5	**6**

Readiness Fundamentals

Note: The child receives one puzzle piece each time a goal is reached.

Bear Puzzle

Mystery Puzzle

Paste puzzle pieces here. Match the numbers.

1	2	3
4	**5**	**6**
7	**8**	**9**

GOOD NEWS FROM SCHOOL

GOOD NEWS FROM SCHOOL

GOOD NEWS FROM SCHOOL

GOOD NEWS FROM SCHOOL

 Readiness Fundamentals

Motor Skills

Children at the readiness level need to work on both gross motor skills using large muscles (hop, skip, run, etc.) and fine motor skills using small muscle groups (use crayons, pencil, scissors, etc.).

Children need to:

- move their bodies in many ways

- locate a distant point and move to it

- move smoothly while holding objects

- be able to roll, throw, and catch

- follow movement directions

- express creativity in movement

- feel and move to a simple beat

- use clay, paint, crayons, etc.

- draw and paint in an age appropriate manner

- begin to use scissors

Watch children as they play outside and work in the classroom. Provide activities to strengthen what they already can do and activities to help develop what they haven't yet mastered.

Section Two includes:
- Teacher instructions and student activities for practicing both gross and fine motor skills.

- Activity sheets for tracing and cutting experiences. (Tracing can be done with: finger, chalk, crayon, or pencil.)

       Readiness Fundamentals

Checking Large Motor Skills

Most of these motions should be done outdoors. You can observe the child at play and check off the ones he/she does successfully, or take the child aside and ask him/her to show you the movement.

									run
									skip
									hop (one foot)
									jump (two feet)
									walk along a line
									walk along a balance beam
									catch a thrown object (beanbag or soft ball)
									throw an object toward a designated spot (beanbag or small ball)
									stand on one foot for several seconds

names

Checking Small Motor Skills

You can observe the child at play and check off the ones he/she does successfully, or take the child aside and ask him/her to do the activity for you.

								string beads on a lace
								tie shoes
								button jacket or sweater
								make a stack of blocks (how many? _____) (how high? _____)
								make a simple picture with: crayon pencil
								cut with scissors: straight line curved line

names

Follow the Footprints

Set-Up

Duplicate the pattern on page 37 on construction paper or lightweight tag. (You may want to make left feet one color and right feet another for those children still confusing the two.)

Place the footsteps on the floor around the classroom. Put the footprints close enough together that children will be able to step from one to the other without having to stretch. Tape them securely to the floor. You don't want them to slip as children are walking.

Have children take turns walking along the footsteps. When they can do it comfortable, challenge them to skip, run slowly, hop on one foot, etc.

Extensions

1. Print letters on the footprints as children are beginning to learn their sounds.

2. Put numbers on the footprints going as high as you wish. 100 is fun if you have room for that many footprints.

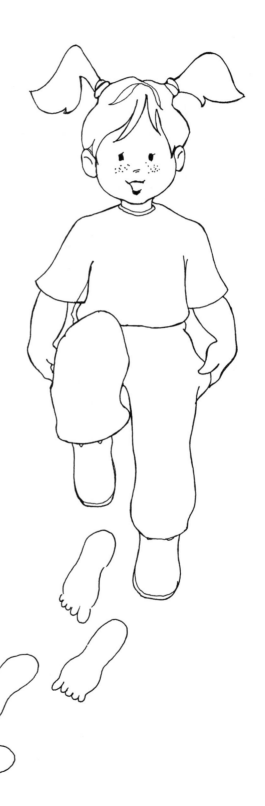

Patterns for "Follow the Footprints"

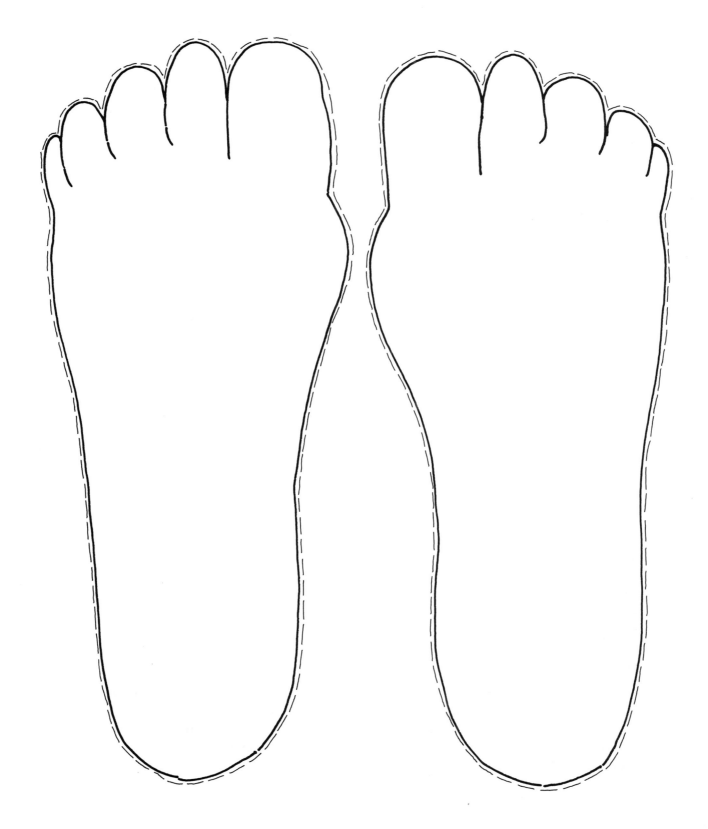

Readiness Fundamentals

Take a "Texture" Walk

Outdoors

Take children around the schoolyard, stopping to touch objects having different textures. Take samples back to the classroom whenever possible.

Touch grass, different types of leaves, gravel, soil, bark of trees, rock and brick walls, etc.

Discuss how the objects feel. Help children express this by modeling words that describe. "This bark feels rough, but this leaf is smooth." "The gravel is bumpy." "These leaves are wet and shiny."

Indoors

Lay out a path of materials with different textures for children to walk on in their bare feet. Be sure the items are securely taped down before children walk on them. You might use carpet squares, fabric such as velvet, corduroy, or burlap, sandpaper in different textures, heavyweight plastic, anything which will not harm their feet, but gives a good tactile experience.

"Feely Box"

Materials
• two boxes with lids
• a variety of fabric scraps

Preparing the Boxes
1. Put fabric samples in the boxes, being sure to include one sample of each fabric in each box. The fabric samples need to be large enough for children to really be able to feel the texture, but small enough to be pulled from the hole in the side.

2. Cut a hole in the side of each box. Make it large enough for a child's arm to comfortable fit through, but not so large they can peek into the box to do the matching activity.

3. Make a big 1 on one box and a big 2 on the other box.

4. Place the lid on each box. You may want to tie it on with string so children won't be tempted to open it to make their matches.

Directions
The child takes a piece of cloth from box number one. He/She feels it carefully, then reaches into box number two and tries to find the same kind of cloth.

Children may work together taking turns making choices or the boxes can be placed in a center for one child to explore.

Developing Fine Motor Skills

Don't begin writing or cutting tasks before children are ready. They will only meet with frustration. Do many large and small muscle activities first.

When children are ready, begin with simple practice activities such as these. Don't rush the process. Allow children to take as long as they need at any stage.

Some of the activities below are described in greater detail on the following pages. In some cases you will find reproducible experiences when provide experience with drawing, coloring, and cutting.

Paint Brushes
Begin with house painting brushes and water. Painting with water on the playground or a large wall allows the child to use his/her whole arm, making large sweeping motions. From there, move to large classroom paint brushes and tempera paint. Painting on large sheets of paper on the floor or an easel helps the child begin to develop more control. Finally have the child paint using a smaller brush for practice in making for fine details in pictures.

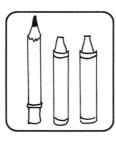

Crayons and Pencils
Have plenty of scrap paper and crayons of different sizes handy. Some children find "fat" crayons easier to handle, others prefer smaller crayons from the beginning. Allow children the opportunity to make any kind of line. Some children will be ready to make an actual picture, others will still be at the scribble stage. Then move on to having children make a specific line or shape. Finally, encourage children to draw a "real" picture.

Repeat the activities with pencils when you feel your students are ready, leading them finally to the point of tracing, copying, and writing letters and numbers.

Scissors
Controlling scissors well enough to make a cut is difficult for many children. These children need time to get used to holding the scissors and making very simple cuts. Provide a stack of newspaper or used computer paper. Let children "fringe" the edges or make any kind of longer cut they feel comfortable with. When they appear successful at random cuts, ask them to make a cut between two lines, then along a specified line. Finally provide art lessons and cut-and-paste tasks requiring specific cuts.

Tracing

As children are ready to begin drawing and writing shapes and letters, some will need greater tactile reinforcement. This can be done using the following items.

Sand
Keep a box or tray of damp (not wet) sand available for children to draw and write in using a finger or small stick.

Sandpaper
Cut shapes, letters, and numbers from sandpaper of various degrees of coarseness. Children trace the sandpaper pieces with a finger.

Glue
Use a white glue to draw shapes and to write letters and numbers on cardboard. You may want to add a bit of food coloring to the glue before using it as the glue becomes clear when it dries. The dry glue gives a smooth, raised shape which children can trace with a finger.

Fingerpaint and Clay

Both fingerpaint and clay offer fun ways to develop small muscle control with the added reward of having a piece of art to take home and share with the family when the activity is over.

Fingerpaint

Don't be deterred by the mess of finger painting. Cover work areas with newspaper, cover children with paint smocks, and have plenty of paper towels handy. A puddle of liquid starch with a little liquid tempera paint makes an inexpensive finger paint.

Pudding mix on a clean table top is the perfect medium for just exploring the feeling of fingerpaint and practicing movements. Be prepared for your students to lick their fingers mid-project. You will probably have a few children who are hesitant to get their hands dirty in the paint. Be patient and keep offering opportunities for them to try.

There are many ways to create a fingerpaint project.

1. Put a puddle of fingerpaint on a sheet of damp fingerpaint paper. Child makes a design on the paper. Encourage swirling movements, but don't be surprised in the beginning when students want to draw in the paint with a finger. When the painting are done, allow them to dry, trim the edges, and mount them on colored construction paper.

2. Put fingerpaint directly on the table top. Create a design. Lay a sheet of paper gently on top to make a print. When the paint is dry, trim the picture and mount it on colored construction paper.

Display finished pictures around the classroom before they are sent home.

Clay

Use any sort of clay - modeling clay, self-hardening clay, or if you have a kiln handy, you can even use firing clay. Give each child a ball of clay about the size of their own fist.

> **Roll** - Have children roll their clay into "snakes." When they have several good "snakes," see if they can shape them into the first letter of their name.

> **Pat** - Have children pat their ball of clay into a flat shape, then use tongue depressors, pencil points, etc. to decorate the piece.

Templates

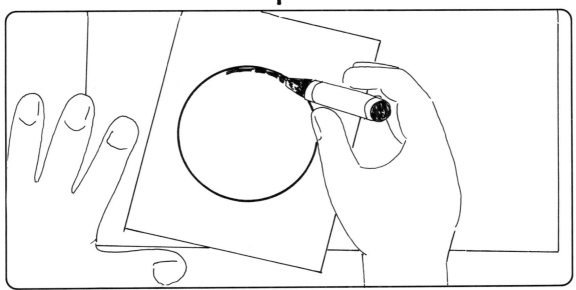

Materials

Reproduce the template patterns on the following page.
Use the shapes as patterns for making a set of templates out of thin cardboard.

    1. Cut the shapes apart along the dotted lines.

    2. Use a mat knife or Exacto knife to carefully cut out the center shapes. Try to keep these in one piece. You will then have two versions of each shape for children to trace - around the outside of one piece and around the inside of the other piece.

    3. Store the shapes in a box or envelope.

How to Use

Children can trace these templates in two different ways.

    1. Trace the outside of the shapes.
    Give children the pieces you cut out of the cards. They lay the shape on a piece of paper and trace around the outside of the cardboard piece.
    They can do this simply as a practice activity using crayons or a pencil, or can trace the shapes several times on drawing paper to create a design.

    2. Trace the inside of the shapes.
    Give children the cards with the centers cut out. They lay the cards on a sheet of paper and trace along the inside opening. Again they can do this as a practice activity or can arrange the shapes to create a design.
    This is a bit more difficult since the card covers up part of the paper.

Variation

Children who are ready for a more advanced activity can use the templates to make designs by rubbing the side of a crayon or piece of chalk from the template to paper to create a colorful design.

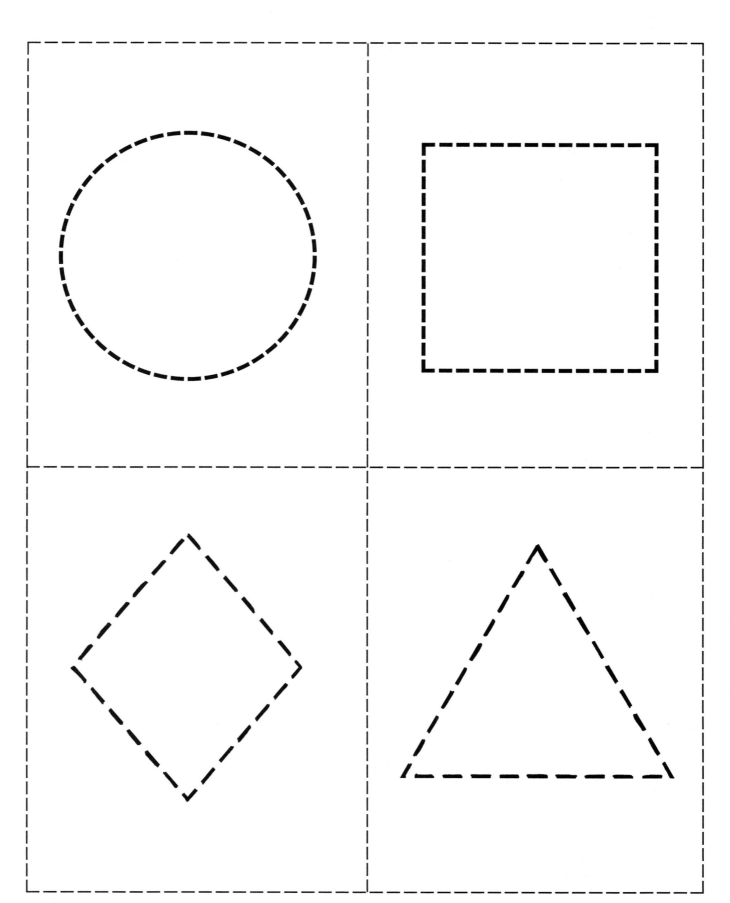

Readiness Fundamentals

Monkey See!
Monkey Do!

This activity can be done in the classroom or on the playground. It makes a great "filler" for any spare minutes you might have and gives children a chance to stretch.

The teacher or a student can act as the leader. Everyone else copies the motions demonstrated. Start with one or two easy movements. Gradually add a greater number and/or more difficult motions to follow.

Here are some suggestions to get you started:

1. Touch different body parts as they are names.

2. Pat your head. (shoulder, knee, waist, toes,etc.)

3. Clasp your hands behind your back, then in front. (show, fast)

4. Wiggle your fingers. (ears, nose, tongue, etc.)

5. Put your arms over your head. (behind your back, at your sides, out from your sides, etc.)

6. Swing your arms together. (forward and back, in opposite directions)

7. Lift one leg. Clap your hands under your lifted leg. Lift your other leg. Clap your hand under it.

8. Bend your left knee and raise your leg behind your back. Tap the shoe on that foot with your right hand.

9. Raise your left knee. Pat it with your right hand. Lift your right knee. Pat it with your left hand.

Pantomime

Show children how to pantomime an action they commonly do. Then have them children act out everyday actions they do at school, at home, or at play. The rest of the class copies the action and tries to guess what the person is doing.

Brush your teeth.

Put on a jacket.

Tie a shoe.

Paint a wall.

Wash a window.

Sweep the floor.

Peel a banana and eat it.

Make an ice cream cone and eat it.

Kick a ball.

Jump to put a ball through the basketball hoop.

Roller skate.

Do a dance.

Jump a rope.

Climb a ladder.

Drive a car.

Dive into water and swim.

Cast a line and catch a fish.

Follow the Leader

Practice gross body movements as you play this old favorite game. Play on a large, grassy or open area. Begin simply. Add more complicated movements when your students are ready. Have children move forward, backward and to either side.

- walk
- run
- gallop
- leap
- tiptoe
- hop on two feet
- hop on one foot
- hop like a frog
- waddle lide a duck
- walk with knees bent

Readiness Fundamentals

With a Hop, Skip, and a Jump!

You will need a large area so children can move freely without bumping into each other. Practice a single movement or a combination of several different moves.

Here are a few examples:

- Walk:

small steps	happy steps
giant steps	sad steps
loud steps	tiptoe steps
quiet steps	backward steps

- Run:

run forward	run with long steps
run backward	run with tiny steps
run in a circle	run-stop-run-stop-run

- Jump:

jump high	jump with hands on hips
jump far	jump with hands over head
jump like a frog	jump up and turn around

- Hop:

hop on one foot	hop forward
hop on two feet	hop backward
hop to the side	hop in a circle

- Skip:

skip forward	skip holding hands with someone
skip slowly	skip with long steps
skip quickly	skip in a circle

- Combination:

  walk — hop on two feet — walk backwards — jump and turn around
  hop on your left foot — hop on your right foot — skip — tiptoe
  run in a small circle — walk backward — jump like a frog
  take three giant steps — run quietly — gallop like a pony

All Aboard the Animal Train

Children form a circle on the carpet or outdoors on the grass. A child is selected to be "IT" and calls out the name of an animal. The children go around the circle moving as they think that animal would move. If a child cannot think of an appropriate motion, select someone to illustrate the action. If no one can decide how to move, the teacher will need to demonstrate an action.

frog	cat	caterpillar
rabbit	crab	elephant
spider	lizard	kangaroo
snake	penguin	monkey
pony	deer	fish
duck	robin	inch worm

Readiness Fundamentals

Obstacle Course

Create a simple path using wide masking tape. This can be done in the classroom or on the playground. Make the obstacle course more or less difficult by adding or removing elements.

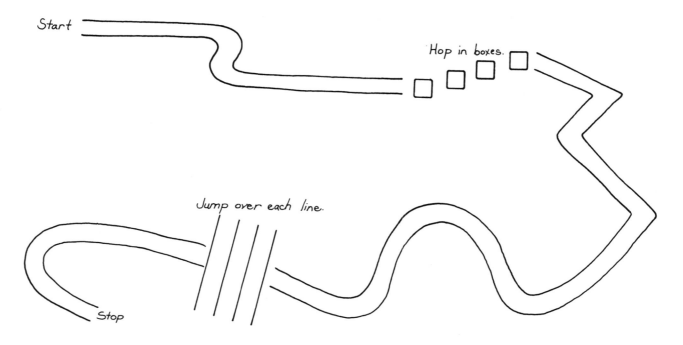

- Children move forward or backward.

- They walk, skip, run, or crawl along the course.

- They may ride tricycles if the path is wide enough.

- Children sit crosslegged in a row when they have completed the obstacle course to wait for directions.

More complicated obstacle courses can be created by adding large wooden blocks (to walk on or step over), cardboard boxes (to step over or crawl through), balance beams, jump ropes, hoops, and classroom furniture (to step up and down on, or to crawl under).

Take advantage of any playground equipment if the obstacle course is outdoors.

 Readiness Fundamentals

Balance Beams

★ Place the board directly on the floor for children with poor balance.

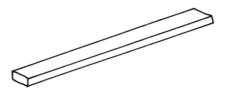

★ Place the board on a stand several inches off the ground when children have developed better balance.

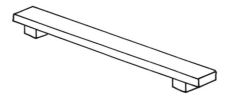

★ Several balance beams can be arranged to form a more complicated challenge.

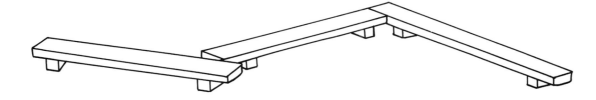

1. Walk straight (arms out for balance)
2. Walk with arms at sides
3. Walk with hands on hips
4. Walk sideways
5. Crawl along the board
6. Walk backward
7. Walk on tiptoes
8. Walk with one foot on the board and one foot off
9. Walk with a beanbag on your head
10. Walk to the center — turn around — go back

Ropes

• Teach children with well-developed motor skills how to jump rope.

• Use jump ropes to create obstacles to move along, around, and over.

Lay a rope along the ground in a straight or wiggly line.

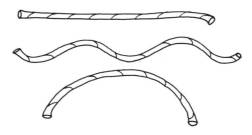

1. Walk/skip/hop along the rope.

2. Walk forward/backward with one foot on each side of the rope.

3. Hop back and forth over the rope using two feet.

4. Hop back and forth over the rope using one foot.

5. Step over the rope; crossing the left foot over to the right side of the rope, then the right foot over to the left side of the rope.

6. Two children swing the rope slowly as a third child hops back and forth over it.

Readiness Fundamentals

Hoops

- Teach children with well-developed motor skills how to use a hoop as a "hula hoop."

- Use hoops to create obstacles to move along, around, and over.

Place one or more hoops on the ground.

1. Walk/skip/hop around the hoop.

2. Walk with one foot in and one foot out of the hoop.

3. Hop in and out of the hoop on two feet/one foot.

4. Place several hoops in a row. Step/hop from one hoop to another.

5. Place several hoops in a scattered pattern. Step/hop from one hoop to another.

6. Swing a hoop over your head; then under your feet. Step through the hoop when it reaches your feet.

Readiness Fundamentals

Beanbags

Beanbag activities help children practice hand-eye coordination as well as work on other motor skills.

Beanbags

1. Toss the beanbag up and catch it.
2. Toss the beanbag up and away from you. Run and catch it.
3. Place the beanbag on your head, back of your hand, or on top of your toes. Walk slowly, then rapidly.
4. Toss the beanbag to a partner.
5. Toss the beanbag at a marker.
6. Create a numbered grid on a large sheet of tag. Each player says which number will be hit and throws the beanbag. If that number is hit, the player gets another turn.

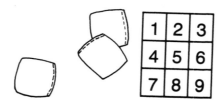

Balls

Students need to have practice in throwing, catching and bouncing balls to develop motor skills and hand-eye coordination.

Balls

These tasks can be made more difficult by using a smaller ball.

1. Roll the ball to a partner.
2. Form a circle and roll the ball back and forth between children.
3. Bounce the ball with two/one hand(s) while standing in one place. Bounce the ball while walking.
4. Throw the ball to a partner.
5. Kick the ball. (Start gently until they can connect with the ball regularly, then try for distance.)
6. Throw the ball at a target on the ground or wall.

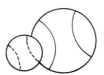

Readiness Fundamentals

Relay Fun

These relays are not done in teams to find a "winner." They are done in single lines or circles to give everyone a change to practice the motor skills involved.

1. From Here to There
Children form one or more lines. The first person in each line goes to a set spot and back again. As each child returns, he/she should go to the back of the line.

2. Delivery Van
Children form one or more lines. The first person in each line is given an object. That person carries the object to a designated place, leaves it, and returns to the line. The second person in each line goes to the object, picks it up, and returns to the line, giving it to the third person. Continue until everyone has had a turn.

3. Over and Under
Children stand in a circle with everyone facing in the same direction. One beanbag or ball is started around.
- Everyone passes it over their heads.
- Everyone passes it betwenn their legs.
- The first person passes it overhead, the second person passes it between the legs, and so on around the circle.

Lace It Up

Lacing requires good small muscle development and eye-hand coordination. Begin with objects containing large holes. Old thread spools or large wooden beads give small hands something to hang on to. Move on to more difficult threading tasks such as lacing a shoe when children are ready.

Create art lessons that require lacing. Make holes with a hole punch. Use real shoe laces (boot length) whenever possible. Dip the tip of a piece of yarn into white glue to create a stiff tip it you are using it for lacing.

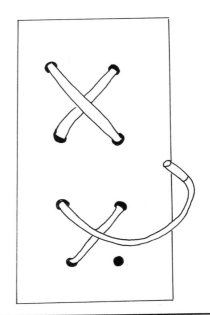

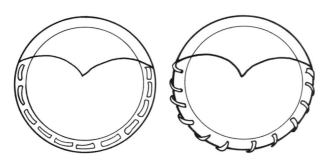

Lace up a heart pocket made from paper plates.

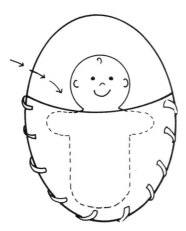

Make a cradleboard for an Indian baby using construction paper. Draw the baby on a small piece of paper. Cut it out and tuck it inside the cradleboard.

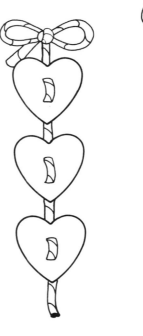 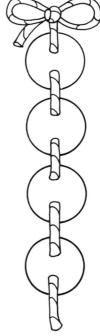

String circles decorated like Christmas ornaments onto a length of yarn.

Finger Plays

Involve children often in the fun and active experience of reciting finger plays. Students physical dexterity is reinforced as well as the development of basic language skills.

The following pages provide a number of finger plays appropriate this this age level. You will find that students never tire of doing these activities. The more familiar the rhyme, the more fun to recite. So share these with children and enjoy.

Count the Balls

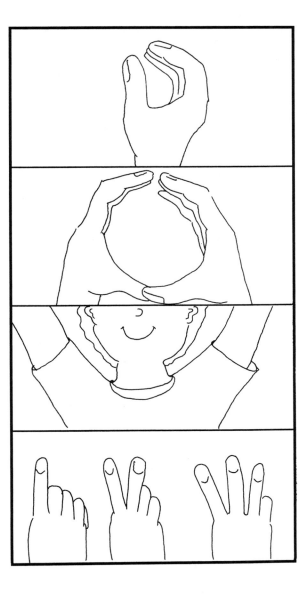

A little ball,

A bigger ball,

A great big ball I see.

Let's count the balls I made.

1, 2, 3.

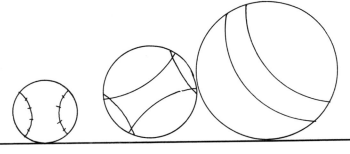

 Readiness Fundamentals

Little Miss Muffet

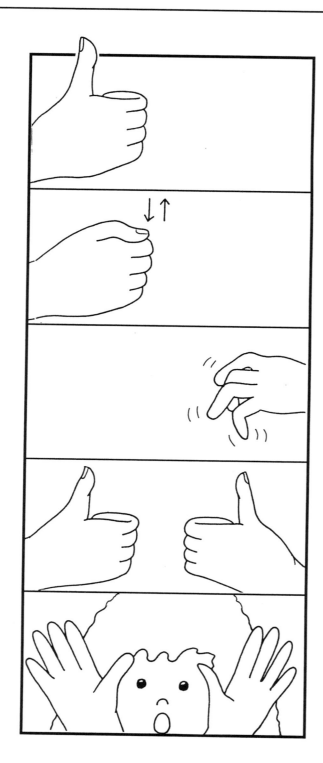

Little Miss Muffet

Sat on a tuffet
Eating her curds and whey.

Along came a spider.

He sat down beside her.

And firghtened Miss Muffet away.

My Family

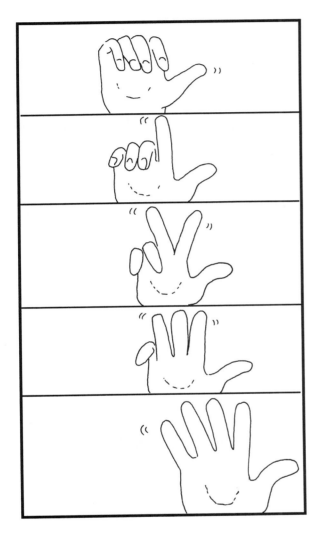

This is my mother.

This is my father.

This is my brother tall.

This is my sister.

This is our baby.

Oh, how I love them all.

Readiness Fundamentals

Mothers Knives and Forks

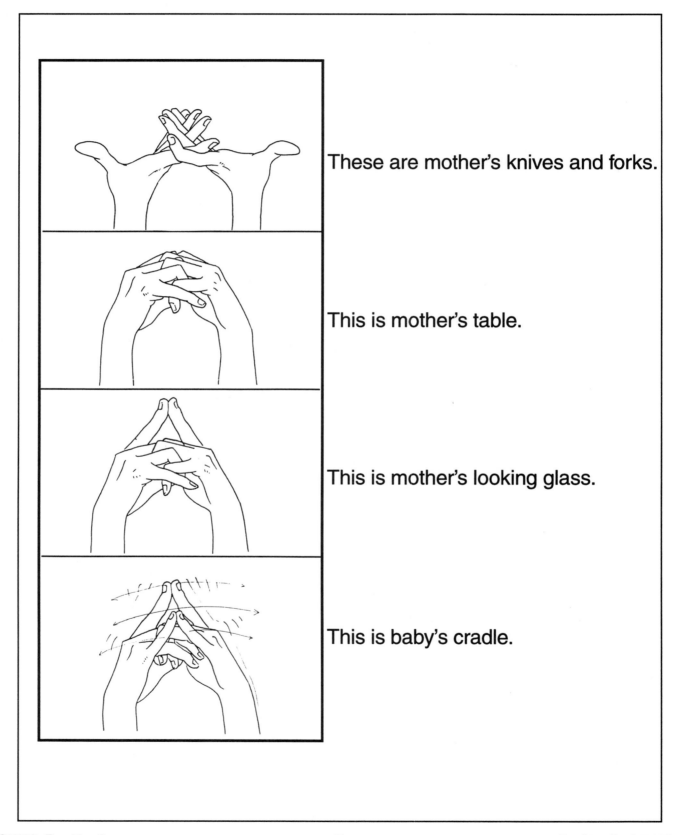

These are mother's knives and forks.

This is mother's table.

This is mother's looking glass.

This is baby's cradle.

Readiness Fundamentals

Action Songs and Games

Children love songs and poems with actions. They provide a positive break when children have been sitting too long. These activities provide practice in listening and motor skills.

- *Where is Thumbkin?*
- *Six little Ducks*
- *Oats, Peas, Beans, and Barley Grow*
- *This Old Man*
- *Head, Shoulders, Knees, and Toes*
- *Whiskey Frisky*

Don't forget to make use of traditional games for developing readiness skills. They provide children with the opportunity to practice motor, listening, sequencing skills. They also develop the spirit of cooperative play.

- *Hokey Pokey*
- *Looby Loo*
- *London Bridge*
- *Did You Ever See a Lassie?*
- *Go In and Out the Window*
- *Drop the Handkerchief*

Check your school music book, any poetry books you may have, and the books in your school library for these and many more.

Did You Ever See a Lassie?

Did you ever see a lassie, a lassie, a lassie, Did you ever see a lassie go this way and that? Go this way and that way, go this way and that way, Did you ever see a lassie go this way and that?

Children form a circle, holding hands. One child is in the center. Children skip around the circle as they sing the first part of the verse. On *"this way and that, "* the person in the center of the circle performs an action. The other children stop circling and imitate the action as they finish sing. The child in the center chooses a new "lassie or laddie," and the game continues.

The Mulberry Bush

Here we go round the mulberry bush, the mulberry bush, the mulberry bush,

Here we go round the   mulberry bush,   So ear-ly in the morning.

(Repeat after each verse.)

1. This is the way we wash our hands, etc.

2. This is the way we brush our teeth, etc.

3. This is the way we comb our hair, etc.

4. This is the way we...
   (Let children make up additional verses.)

Children form a circle. They skip around the circle
holding hands as they sing. They act out the activity
sung about in each verse.

A good source for action songs and games is the **Wee Sing and Play** series by Pamela
Conn Beall and Susan Hagen Nipp; Price/Stern/Sloan Publishers, 1985.

Swimming, Swimming

[1]Swim - ming, swim - ming [2]in the swim - ming hole, -- When [3]days are hot, when [4]days are cold, [5]in the swim-ming hole.--

[6]Breast stroke, [7]side stroke, [8]fan - cy div - ing, too. --

[9]Don't you wish you ne - ver had an-y-thing else to do: [10]BUT

Motions:
1. Do overarm "crawl" motions to each beat.
2. Hold arms out like a big hole.
3. Wave hands in front of face like a fan.
4. Pretend to shiver with cold.
5. Hold arms out like a hole.
6. Pretend to do the breast stroke.
7. Pretend to do the side stroke.
8. Hold nose and make other hand dive down.
9. Point finger down on each beat moving from left to right.
10. Shout "BUT!"

Painting

Turn your students loose on the playground (within limits of course) with paint brushes (house-painting size on down) and buckets of water. (Keep plenty of paper towels around! You may want to ask parents to help by sending in one roll of towels each.) Let them stretch their imaginations for a while; then set specific tasks.

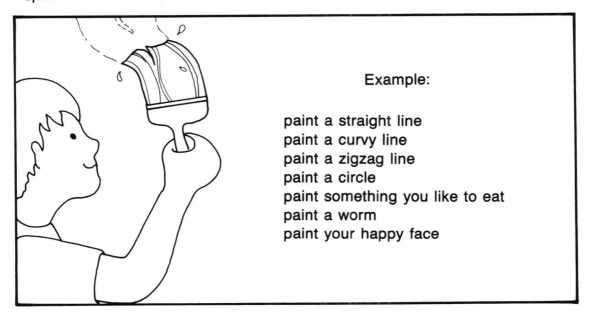

Example:

paint a straight line
paint a curvy line
paint a zigzag line
paint a circle
paint something you like to eat
paint a worm
paint your happy face

Regular classroom size paint brushes require finer muscle control. Spread out large sheets of butcher paper. Give each child a brush and container of paint. (You may want to do this activity in small groups.) Have the children follow specific directions.

1. Use the examples from above.
2. Teacher paints a design for the children to copy.

Keep a paint center in your class at all times for children to experiment with color and to create their own "masterpieces."

Oh, Were They Ever Happy by Peter Spier; Doubleday & Company, Inc., 1978 is a delightful story about children and paint. Read it to your class on a day when you all need a good chuckle.

Using Activity Sheets
Pages 69 to 88

The activities in this section each contain a reproducible page which can be done at many levels of sophistication,

- **following along with a finger**
- **using a "fat" crayon or piece of chalk**
- **using a pencil**
- **using scissors**

★ Pages 69 to 82 are tracing experiences of various kinds:
- staying between lines of various widths
- staying on straight lines
- staying on curved lines
- tracing shapes to complete a picture

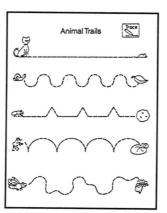

★ Pages 83 to 88 require children to cut and paste. Be sure your students are ready to cut both straight and curving lines before asking them to do these tasks.

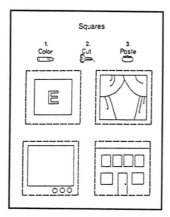

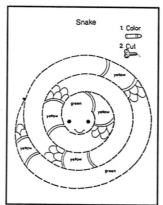

Here We Go...

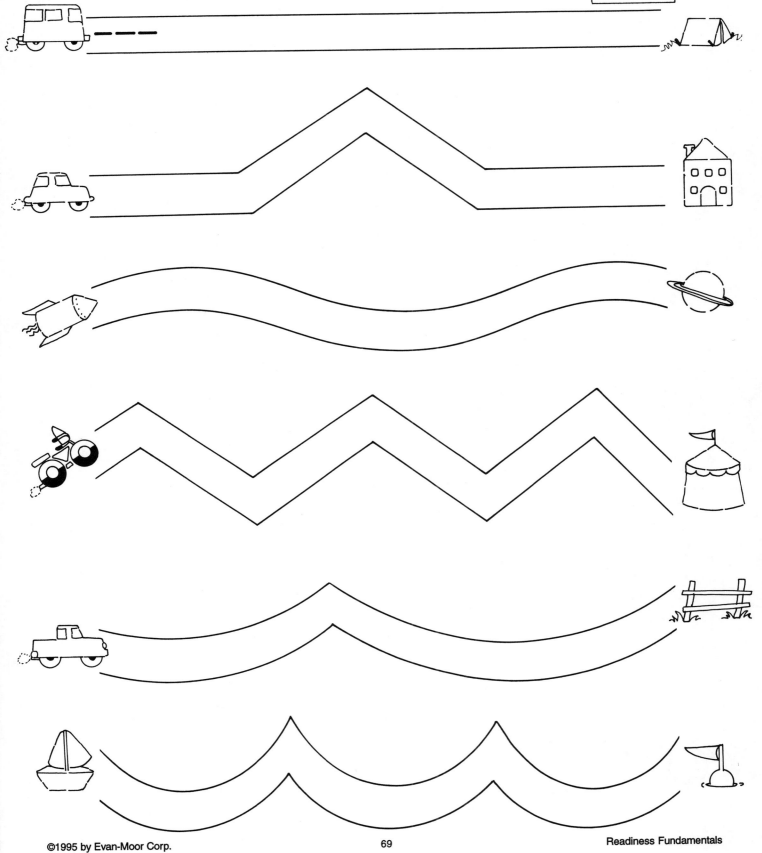

Animal Trails

Readiness Fundamentals

Creepy Crawlers

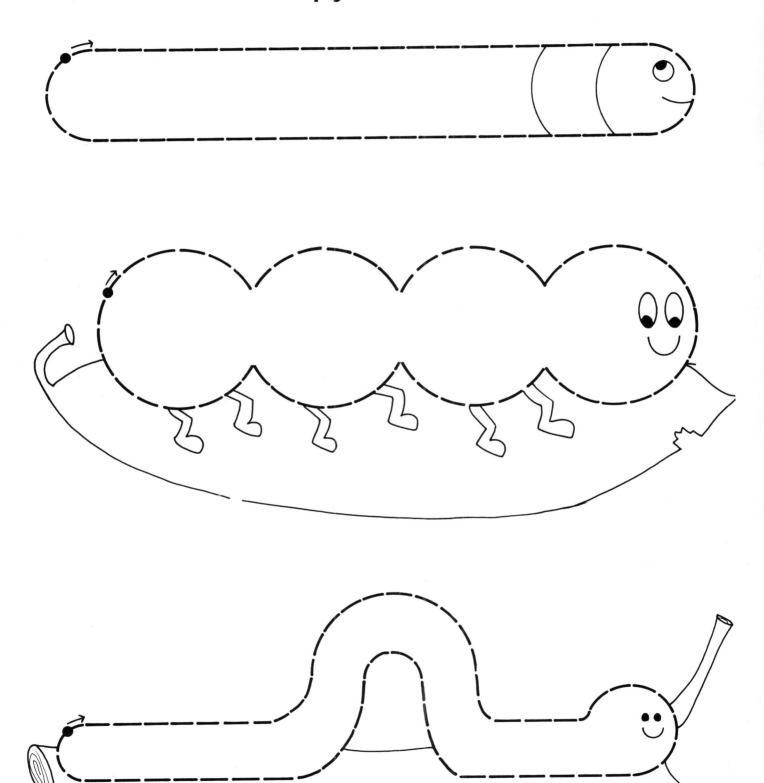

The Nest

Help the hen find her nest.

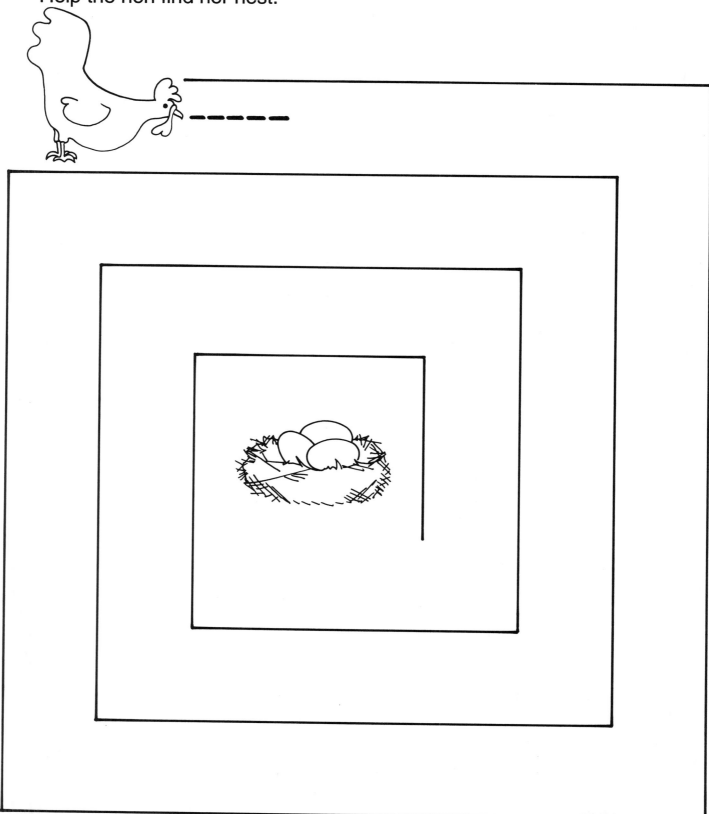

The Bone

Help the dog find his bone.

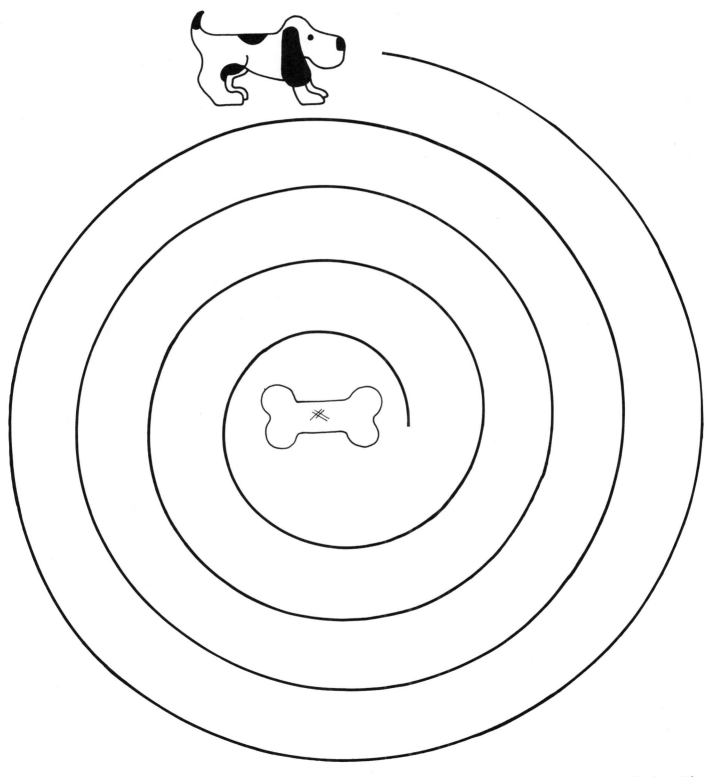

Readiness Fundamentals

Teacher: Children trace and color the picnic food.

Picnic Time

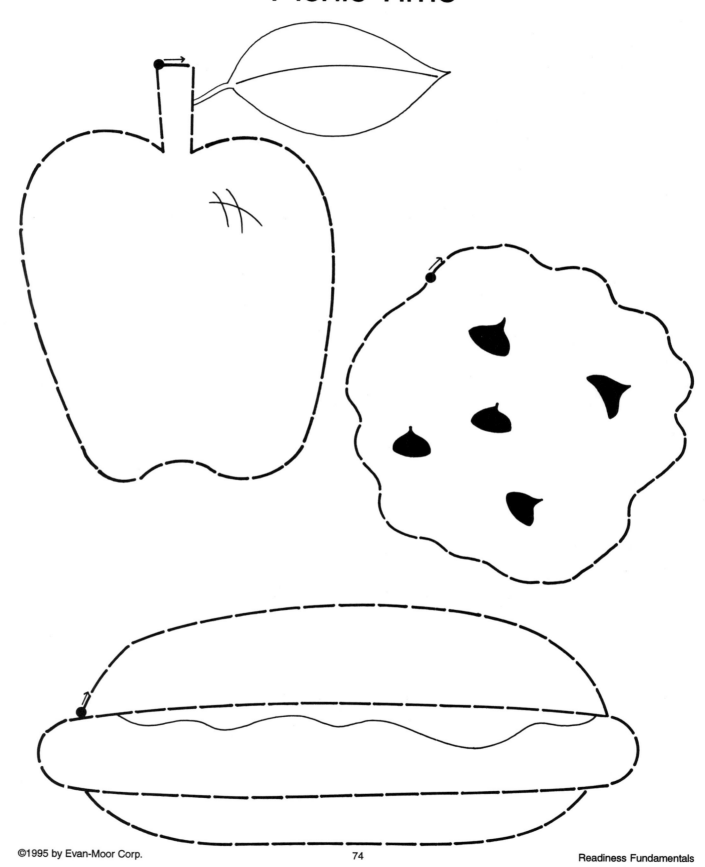

Trace the Shape

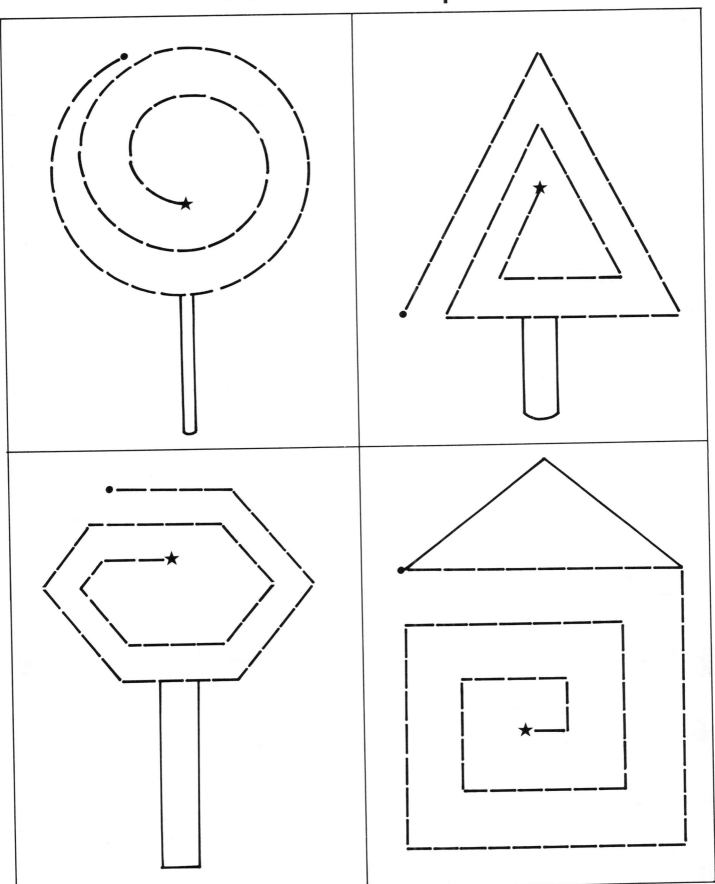

Readiness Fundamentals

Start at the ☆ .

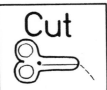
Cut

☆ _____

☆ _____

☆ _____

☆ _____

Start at the 🍎 .

Readiness Fundamentals

Teacher: Children are to cut on the lines.

Start at the  .

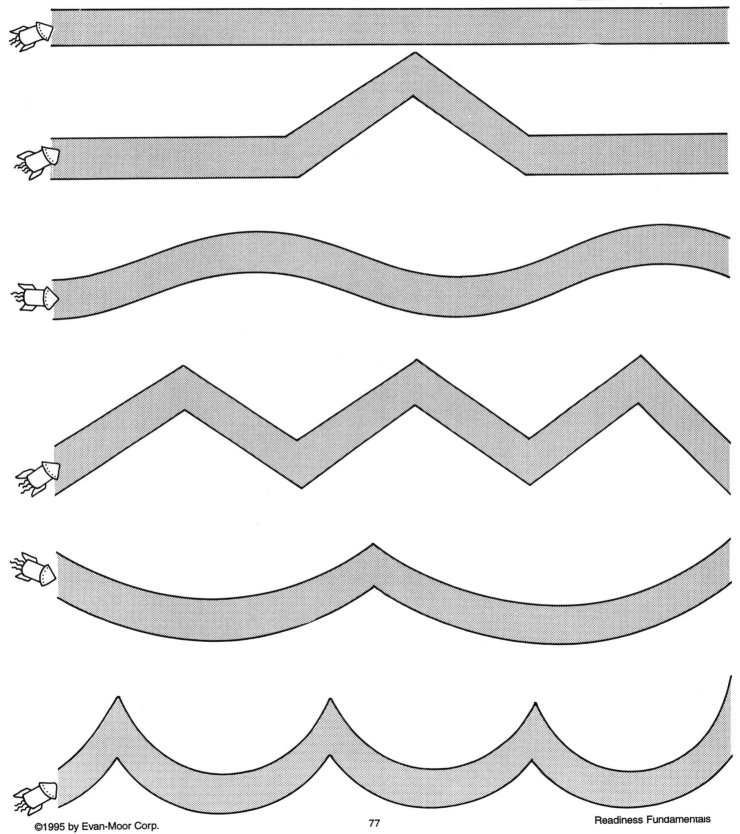

77
Readiness Fundamentals

Follow the Dots

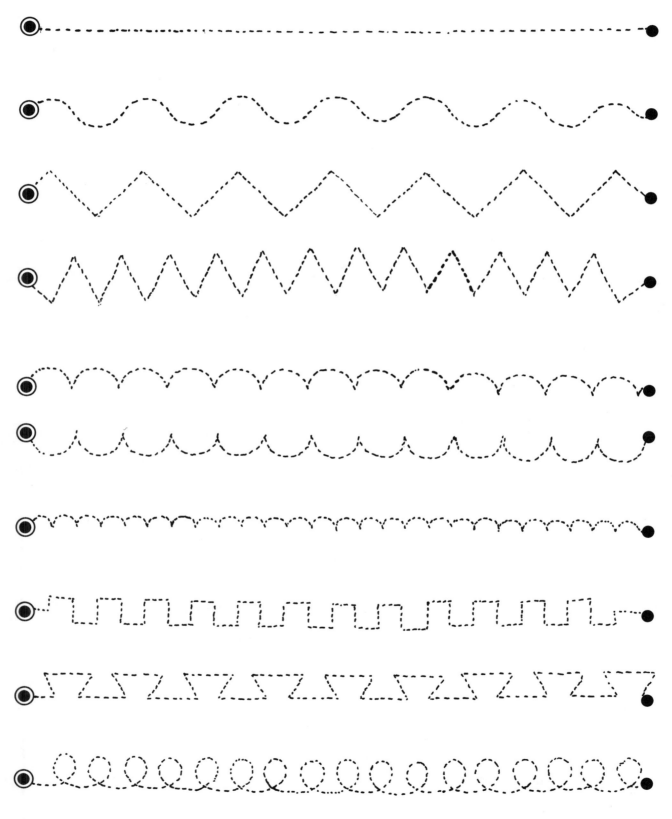

Finish the Ladders

Put the rungs on these ladders, but always go left to right.

Readiness Fundamentals

Finish the Train Tracks

While drawing the ties to connect the tracks, always go down - never up.

1. Trace

2. Color

Ladybugs

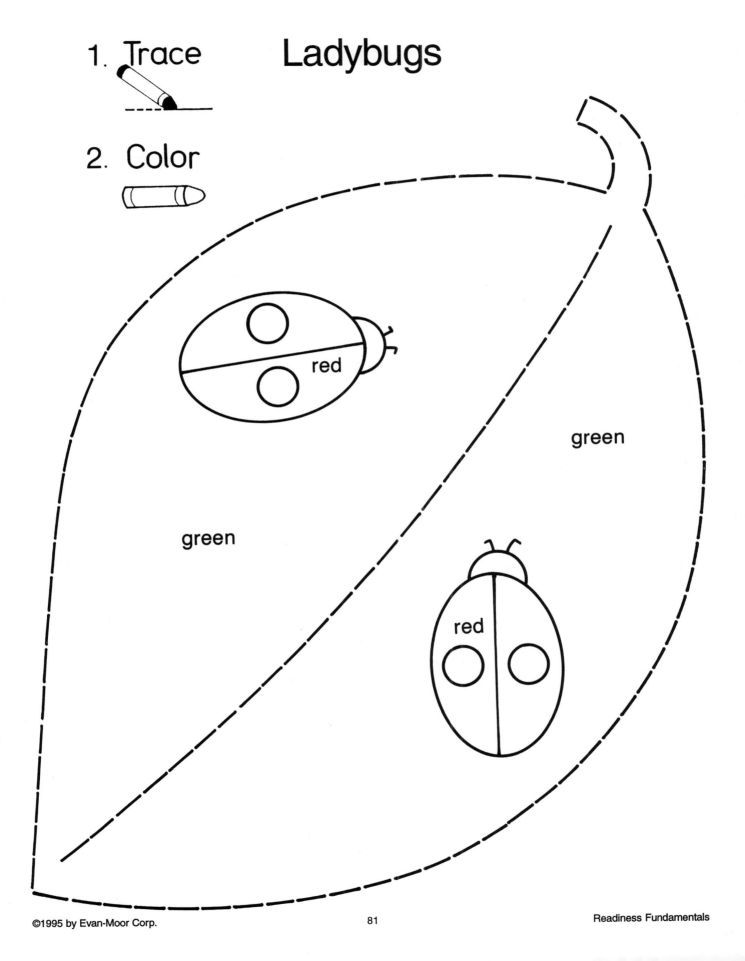

red

green

green

red

Snail

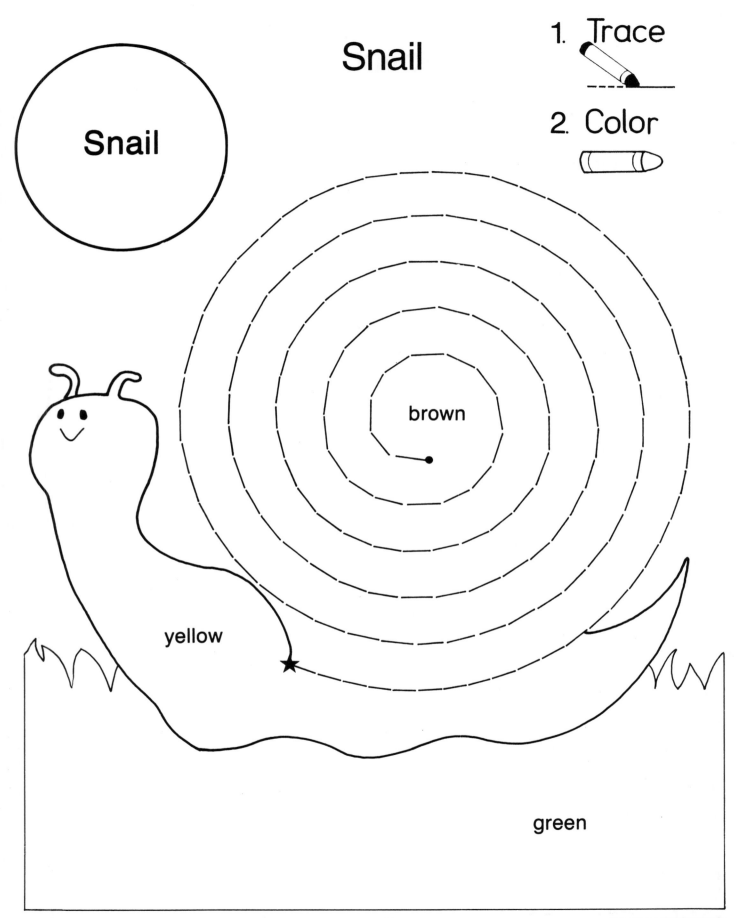

Snail

1. Trace

2. Color

brown

yellow

green

82

Readiness Fundamentals

Squares

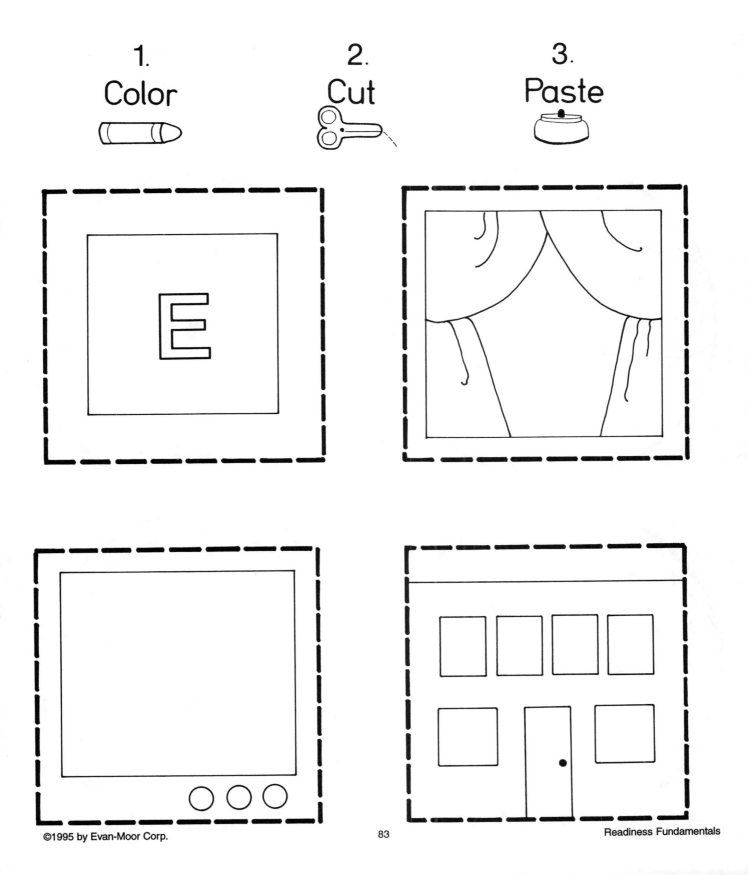

1. Color

2. Cut

3. Paste

Readiness Fundamentals

Circles

1.
Color

2.
Cut

3.
Paste

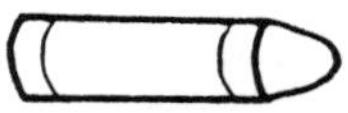

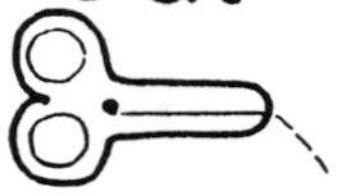

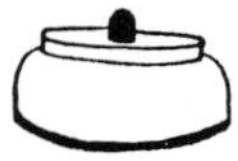

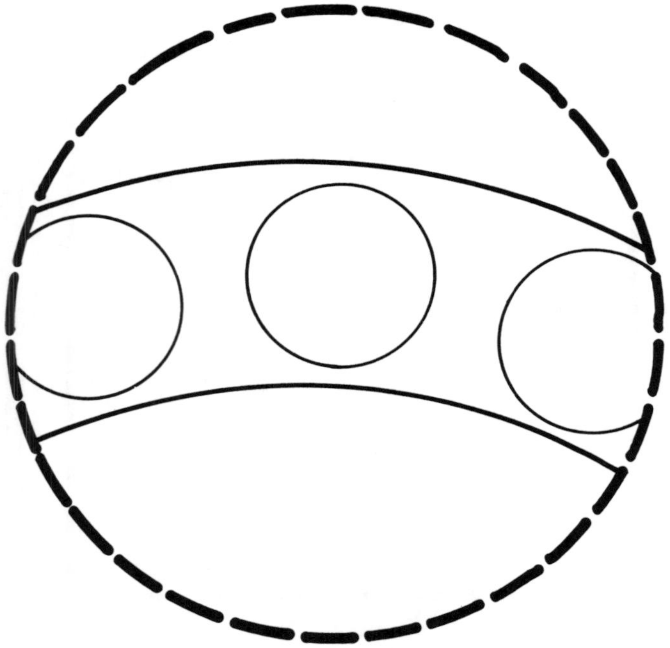

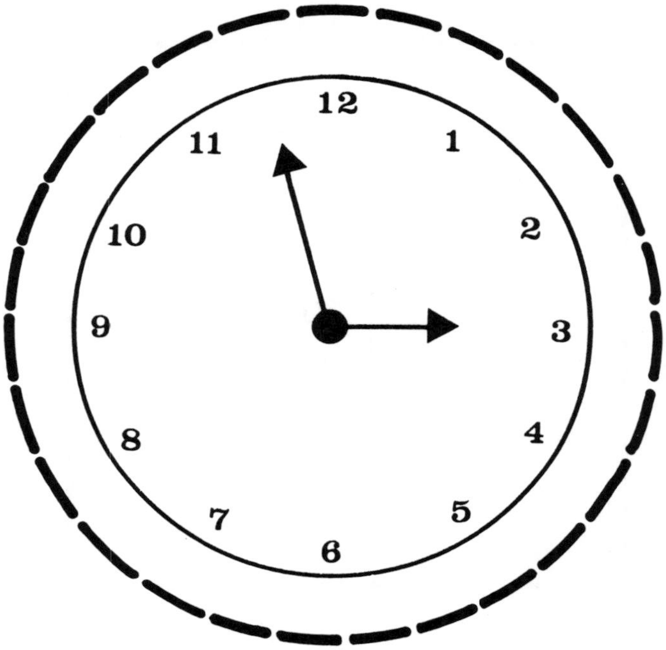

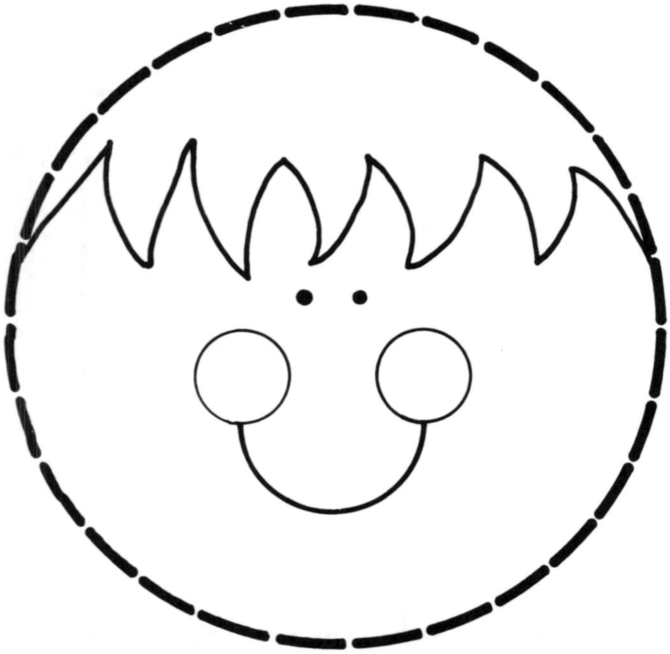

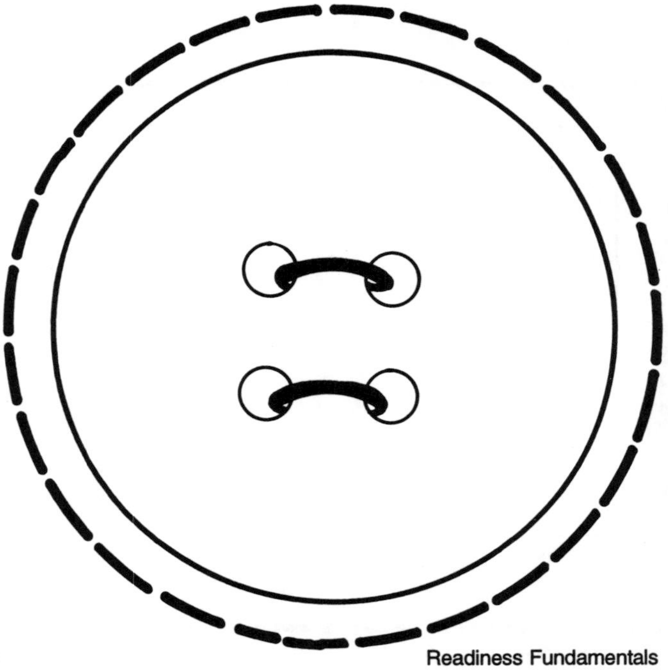

12
11   1
10   2
9   3
8   4
7   5
6

84

Teacher: You may add a 12'' piece of yarn to the snake's head and hang it in your classroom.

Snake

1. Color

2. Cut

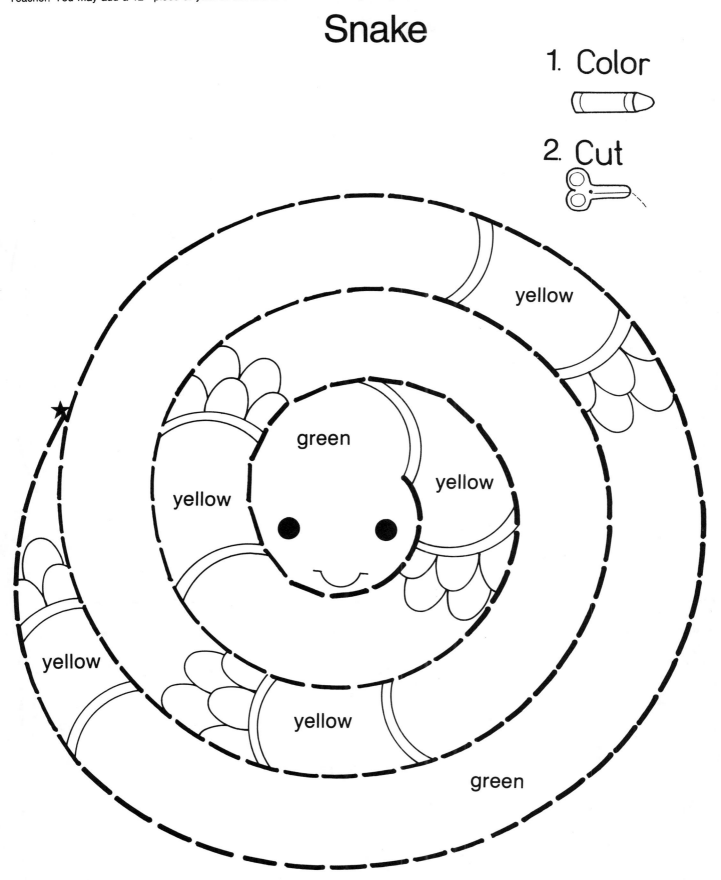

yellow

green

yellow

yellow

yellow

yellow

green

85

Readiness Fundamentals

Teacher: Have children cut out the fish and paste them in the fish bowl.

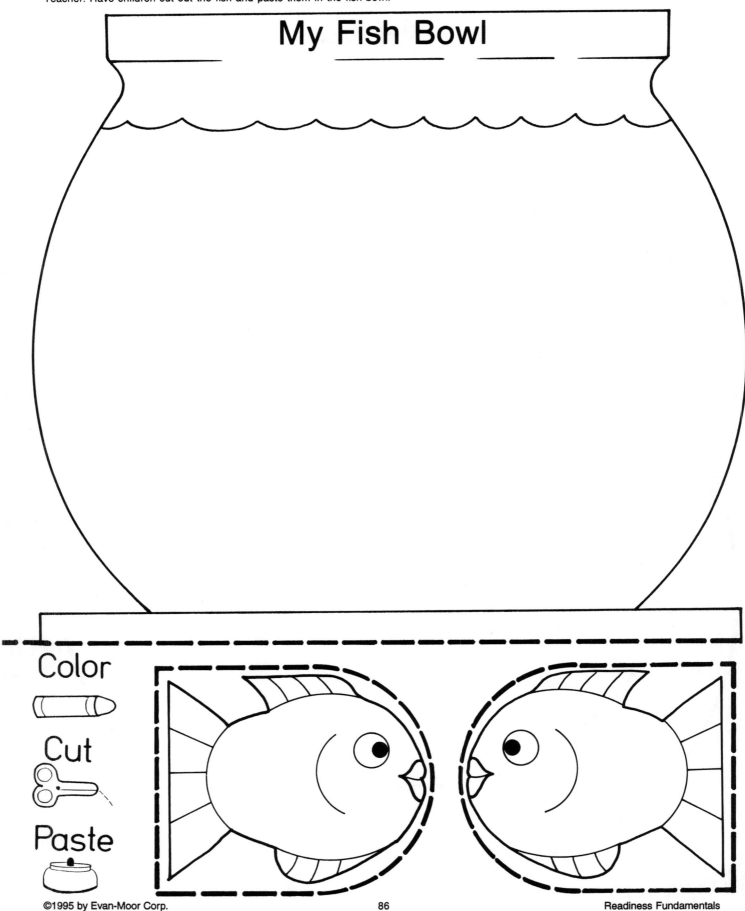

My Fish Bowl

Color

Cut

Paste

Readiness Fundamentals

Teacher: Have children cut out the spiders and paste them on the web.

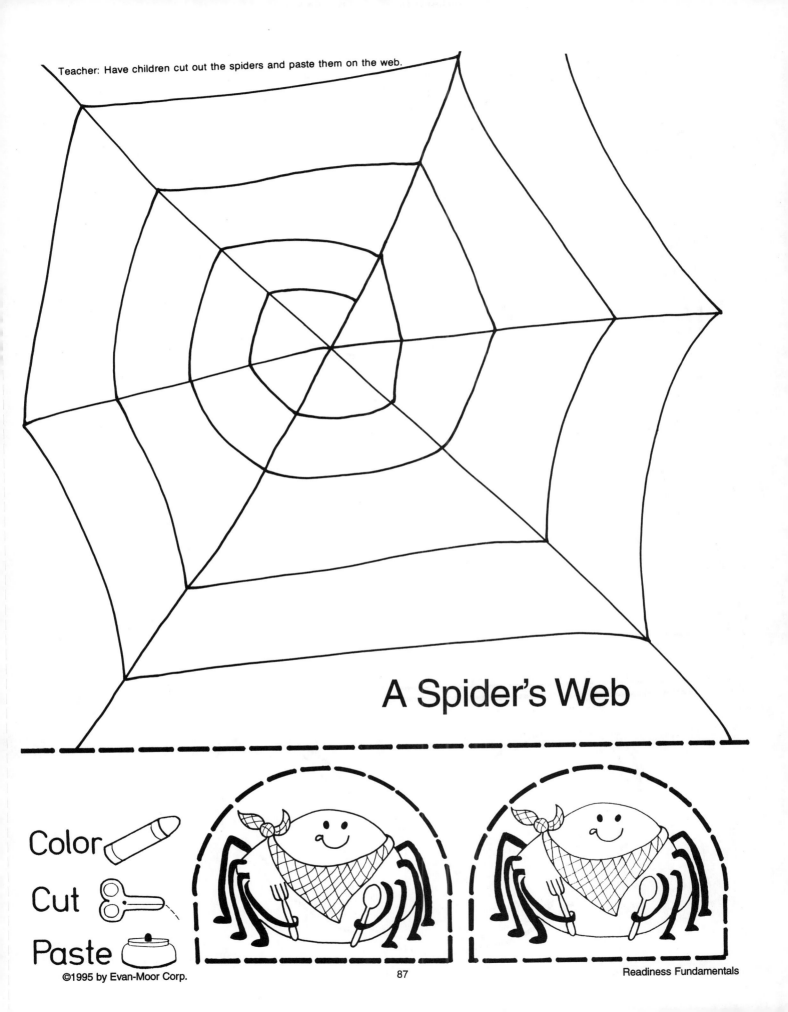

A Spider's Web

Color

Cut

Paste

Readiness Fundamentals

Teacher: Have children cut out the cat and the tail. Paste the tail to the circle on the cat's back.

My Pet Cat

1. Color
2. Cut
3. Paste

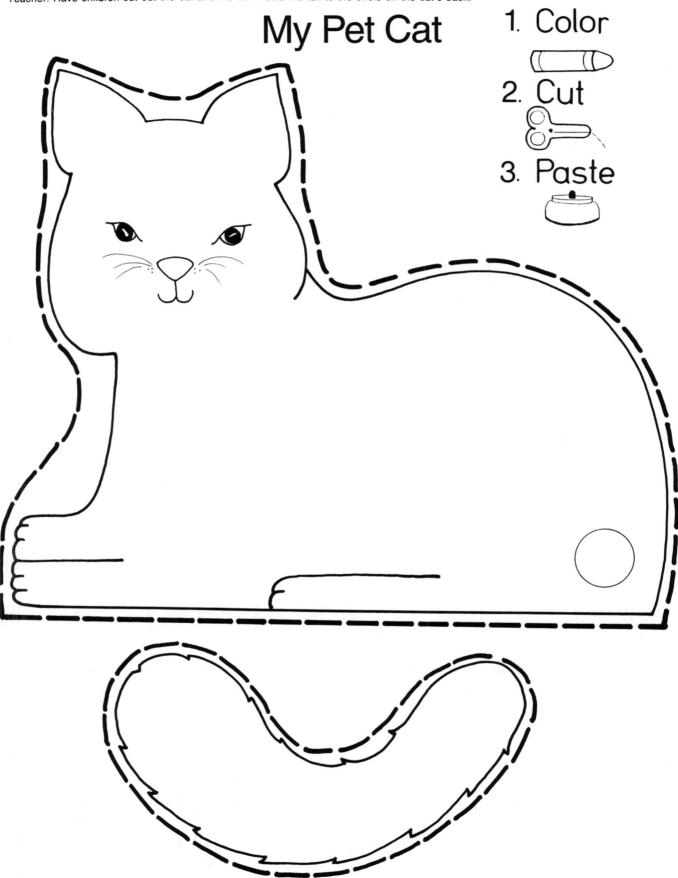

Listening Skills

We can't assume that all children come to school with good listening
habits. Listening carefully for a specific purpose requires much practice.
Children who have a rich background of language and experiences,
plus good listening skills have an easier time learning in a classroom
situation.

Section three provides activities to help children...
- improve their listening skills
- follow oral directions
- listen to others in a conversation situation
- recognize rhythm in music and poetry

Section three provides a variety of techniques for teaching listening skills including:
- using games and songs
- dramatic play
- movement activities
- using stories and poetry
- using reproducible pages

The reproducible pages in this section provide practice for children ready to do paper
and pencil types of tasks. Each page requires careful listening. The activities require
children to mark, color, draw, or fold according to oral directions.

Each of these pages also includes an extension activity for practicing the same skill
without the use of paper and pencil.

                                       Readiness Fundamentals

Listening to Common Classroom Directions

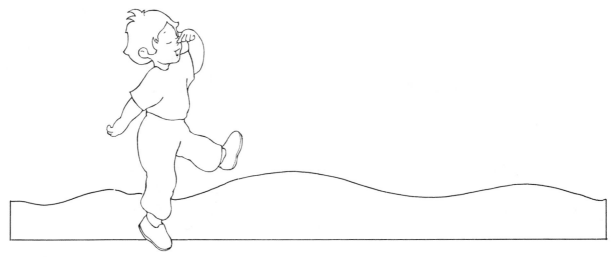

Make a list of the common oral directions you use in your classroom. Add any non-verbal clues you use for the same purposes (hand signals, bell, etc.). Provide practice in following these directions as a listening game early in the year. Any time it seems children are forgetting or not listening, repeat the game.

Following Directions

1. Give each direction separately for children to follow. Do each direction several times. Don't do the whole list at one time in the beginning.

"Stand up."
"Sit down."
"Line up by the door."
"Look at me and listen."
"Fold your hands."
"Put your _____ away."
"Come to your table and sit down."
"Take out your _____."

2. Once they show they can do each individual direction, go through the directions giving two, then three at a time. Ask one child at a time to do the activity at first, then a whole table, and finally the whole class.

"Stand up and push your chair up to the table."
"Go to the rug, sit down, fold your hands in your lap."

3. Practice more complicated directions involving other materials and people.

"Please put the toy truck on the bottom shelf."
"Write your name on your paper."
"Please take this note to the librarian."

The Echo Game

Explain what an echo does. Children are to "echo" back the work, phrase, sentence, or verse you say. This can be done as whole group or by individual children.

Words and Number

a a o

e e i i e

bu-bu-boo

2 4 6 8

9 6 3 0

0 3 5 7 8

caterpillar

hip-hip-hippo

abracadabra

Phrases

cats and dogs

pickle juice for pigs

wiggly whiskers

elephant toes

teeny, tiny tadpoles

six silly sailors

Sentences

Bill ran to the ballpark.

Karen wanted cotton candy.

Will the wind blow my kite to the moon?

Mary made milkshakes on Monday morning.

Susie sews shirts for seasick sailors.

Verses

Dickery, dickery dare,

The pig flew up in the air;

The man in brown soon brought him down,

Dickery, dickery dare.

Clapping Rhymes

A Big Family

❊   ❊
Fa - ther and Mo - ther

❊   ❊
Sis - ters and bro - ther

❊   ❊
Two grand - fa - thers

❊   ❊
And one grand - mo - ther

Wait!
There's more!

❊   ❊
Lots of Aunt - ies

❊   ❊
Lots of Un - cles

❊   ❊
Cou - sins, cou - sins

❊   ❊
By the do - zens

A Little Family

❊   ❊
My mom and me

❊   ❊
Just two to see

❊   ❊   ❊
Hap - py as can be!

Readiness Fundamentals

Clap Your Hands, Snap Your Fingers

The teacher demonstrates the pattern to be followed. Children repeat the pattern. This can be done as a rhythmic activity alone or to accompany a verse or song.

A. Repeat the pattern:

    1. clap snap clap snap clap snap...

    2. clap clap snap clap clap snap...

    3. snap snap snap clap snap snap snap clap...

    4. clap snap clap snap clap clap clap...

    5. clap clap snap clap clap snap clap clap snap snap clap clap snap...

    6. clap snap clap clap snap snap clap clap clap snap snap snap...

B. With a poem or song:

    Jack be nimble, Jack be quick,

    Jack jump over the candlestick.

C. To accompany practice of a skill:

    Clapping a rhythm is perfect with counting practice.

    5   10   15   20   25   30   35   40   45   50

Hear and Feel the Beat

Children will each need two rhythm sticks (pencils or tongue depressors can be used as substitutes). The teacher can be the leader in the beginning. Later a student volunteer can be the leader.

These activities become progressively more difficult. Don't move to the next level until your children are comfortable with the first one.

1. Children follow the tapping pattern given by the leader.
Start simple, work toward more complicated patterns.
Tell the pattern and model it, then have children follow.

- Tap the floor (two times, 4 times, etc.).
- Tap the desk.
- Tap high.
- Tap low.
- Tap in front of you.
- Tap in back of you.

2. Partner Sticks
Two students face each other and both tap.

- Tap the floor two times.
- Tap your own sticks together two times.
- Tap your partner's sticks two times.

Repeat the pattern.

3. Put on a favorite piece of music and tap a pattern along with it.

Rhythm Sticks

Use purchased sticks or make your own from dowling or pieces of bamboo. Be sure to sand the ends to prevent splinters.

x = tap
— = rest

Copy the pattern:

1. X - X - X - X -...

2. X X - X X - X X...

3. X - - X - - X - -...

4. X - X X - X X X...

5. X - - - X - - - X X X...

6. X X X - X X - X - X X - X X X

Tap out the beat to a favorite poem or song:

x   x   x   x x   x   -
Twin-kle, twin-kle lit-tle star,

x x x   x   x   x   x   -
How I won-der what you are!

x x x   x   x   x   x   -
Up a-bove the world so high,

x x x   x   x   x   x   -
Like a dia-mond in the sky.

x   x   x   x x x   x   -
Twin-kle, twin-kle lit-tle star,

x   x x   x   x   x   x
How I won-der what you are!

Stop, Listen, Go

Children listen to your oral directions. They then do the action or series of actions you describe. This can be done in the classroom or outdoors. This is an opportunity for children to practice their motor skills as well as good listening.

Give the directions orally. Demonstrate actions only if children are having difficulty understanding the directions.

1. Touch your head, knees, and toes.

2. Clap your hands behind your back, over your head, and in front of your body.

3. Hop up and down five times; then turn around.

4. Lift your leg and clap your hands underneath. Lift your other leg and clap under it.

5. Hop around in a little circle on one foot.

6. Swing one arm to the front and the other arm to the back.

7. Squat down and walk like a duck.

8. Pretend you are a bird and fly around the room. Don't bump into anyone.

9. Stand on one foot and touch your nose with your finger.

10. Raise one foot behind your back and touch your shoe.

At the Animal Fair

A. Practice the sounds various animals make.

cat	chicken	duck
dog	rooster	pigeon
lamb	horse	lion
cow	mule	frog
pig	turkey	snake

B. The teacher makes a sound. The children name the animal.

C. The teacher names an animal. The children make the sound.

D. Give each child (or group of children) a picture or headband showing an animal. Tell a familiar story such as *Henny Penny*. Every time the child's character is named in the story, the child stands up and makes the animal's sound.

Readiness Fundamentals

Listen....then Move

Play games where children are required to listen carefully
to directions in order to know how and when to move.

Mother May I?

Children stand in a row facing the person who is giving the directions. This person (mother or father) calls a name and gives a simple direction. "Sally. Take two giant steps." The child called on must ask "Mother (or Father), may I?" before moving. Mother answers "Yes you may," and the child called on can move. If the child moves before asking for permission, he/she must go back to the starting line. The first person to reach mother is the winner.

Red Light, Green Light

Children stand in a row facing one person. This person represents the traffic light. When the "light" says green, players move forward. When the "light" says red, the players must stop. Anyone who moves after the light says red must return to the starting point. Select how the children are to move before starting the game (walk, tiptoe, run, skip). The first person to reach the traffic light is winner.

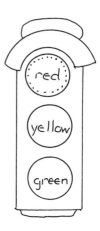

Horse Feathers

Children will need to understand that only birds have feathers and to know the names of several birds before playing this game.

Children form a circle. "IT" stands in the center. (This may need to be the teacher.) Children skip around the circle as long as "IT" names animals that do have feathers (robin feathers, chicken feathers, eagle feathers). They squat down whenever "IT" names something that does *not* have feathers (horse feathers, elephant feathers). Someone left standing at the wrong time is chosen to become "IT."

Let's Play a Game

Verbal games require good listening skills and auditory memory. Here are some simplified versions of some old favorites. You may need to play them in small groups.

I Spy

Set a few requirements to follow in choosing an item. Example:

> The item must be in full sight.
> It must be something children can name.
> It must be clearly described.

One person is selected to be "IT." This person selects an item and describes it. The other children try to guess what it is. (Have children raise their hands before guessing so that everyone can have a chance.) A person giving a correct answer becomes "IT."

Grandma's Trunk

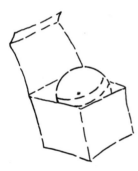

The teacher starts by saying, "I am going on a trip and I'm taking my grandma's trunk. I am packing my (shoes)." The first child repeats what the teacher packed and adds one item. "I am packing my shoes and my (nightgown)." Continue around the group until everyone has had a turn.

Variations:

I am putting my (ball) in my toy box.
I am putting (carrots) in my soup.
I am taking (cookies) on the picnic.

Hide and Seek

One child leaves the room. An object is hidden somewhere in the classroom. The child returns. Clues are given orally. (Have a different child give each clue.) Continue playing until the object is found.

Example:

Clue 1 It is in a box.
Clue 2 The box is under a table.
Clue 3 The table is in the back of the room.

Readiness Fundamentals

Action Songs

Learning the lyrics and melody to a new song requires careful listening. Add the element of actions to perform and you have an excellent way to promote good listening skills while having fun.

Hokey Pokey

You put your right hand in, you put your right hand out,
You put your right hand in and you shake it all about,
You do the hokey pokey, and you turn yourself around,
That's what it's all about!

2. You put your left hand in...
3. You put your right foot in...
4. You put your left foot in...
5. You put your right shoulder in...
6. You put your left shoulder in...
7. You put your right hip in...
8. You put your left hip in...
9. You put your head right in...
10. You put your back right in...
11. You put your whole self in...

Children stand in a circle. They perform each action as they sing the song. They clap the beat each time when singing "That's what it's all about."

         Readiness Fundamentals

Where's the Bear

Use the bear stick puppet to play "*Where's the bear?*" Children will be practicing listening to follow directions at the same time they develop a greater vocabulary of positional words.

Getting Ready
Give each child a copy of the bear on page 102.
- Color the bear.
- Cut the puppet out following the dotted lines.
- Fold the bear in half along the center line.
- Tape the bear to a tongue depressor and paste two ends together.

Playing "Where's the Bear":
Have children take their stick puppets. Give an oral direction telling him/her where to put the puppet. Use a variety of different positional words as you give directions such as:

> "Put the bear under your chin."
> "Hold your bear in your right hand."
> "Put the bear between your knees."
> "Hold your bear behind your back."

Adjust the difficulty of the language and the task to the maturity and language development of your students.

Variation
Use other objects to play the game. For example, small objects such as a pencil, thread spool, rock, etc.

Note: Reproduce this form to make sticks puppets to use with "Where's the Bear?" on the preceding page.

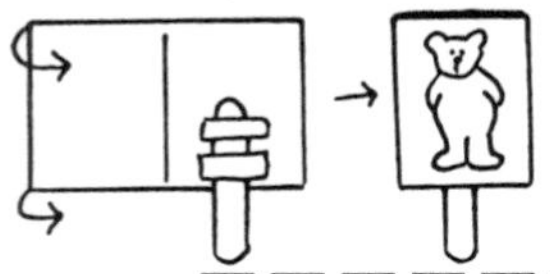

Let's Take a Listening Walk

Take advantage of pleasant days to practice listening skills out in the fresh air.

Choose a location for the walk.

1. neighborhood
2. a business area
3. a local park
4. a zoo or animal shelter
5. around the school buildings

Set a listening task.

1. animal sounds
2. sounds people make
3. vehicle sounds
4. work sounds
5. weather sounds

Enjoy the walk. Discuss what was heard when you return to the classroom.

Readiness Fundamentals

What is in My Basket?

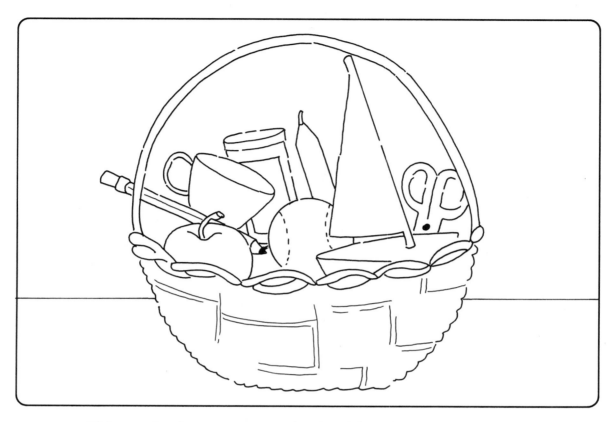

This can be done as a supervised activity with a small group
of children or as an independent activity in a center.

You will need:
    a blindfold
    12 small jars with lids

Fill two jars 1/2 full with each of these items:
    beans   cotton puffs
    marbles   nails
    rice   tooth picks

The child should shake each jar to hear what sound it makes. Then:
    1. Put on the blindfold.
    2. Shake the jars. Find two that sound alike.
    3. Take off the blindfold to see if he/she is correct.

 Readiness Fundamentals

Classroom Sounds

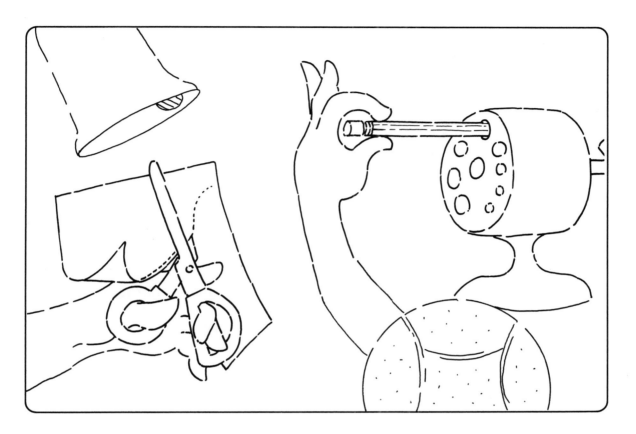

Make sounds that are commonly heard in a classroom. Children have to decide what is making the sound.

close the door
bounce a ball
write on the chalkboard
sharpen a pencil
walk around the room
turn the pages of a book

move a chair
pour water
tear paper
sneeze
cough
laugh

What Do I Hear?

A Listening Center

This can be done as a supervised activity with a small group of children or as an independent activity in a center.

You will need:
    a blindfold
    12 small jars with lids

Fill two jars 1/2 full with each of these items:
beans	cotton puffs
marbles	nails
rice	toothpicks

The child should shake each jar to hear what sound it makes. Then:
    1. Put on the blindfold.
    2. Shake the jars. Find two that sound alike.
    3. Take off the blindfold to see if he/she is correct.

1   2   3

 Readiness Fundamentals

Where Am I?

A child is chosen to be "IT" and sent out of the room. The rest of the children are scattered around the room with some sitting and some standing up. "IT" is blindfolded and brought into the classroom. "IT" calls a child's name. The child answers with "Where am I?" "IT" has to tell if the child is sitting down or standing up and where he is in the classroom (back, front, by the windows, etc.). If "IT" is correct, they change places. If "IT" is wrong, he calls another child's name and tries again.

Readiness Fundamentals

The Fox and the Hen

Two children are chosen to be the fox and the hen. They leave the room. While they are gone, three children are selected to be chicks. All children put their heads down. The fox and the hen come in. The three chicks begin to "peep" calling for their mother. The hen tries to find the chicks before the fox does.

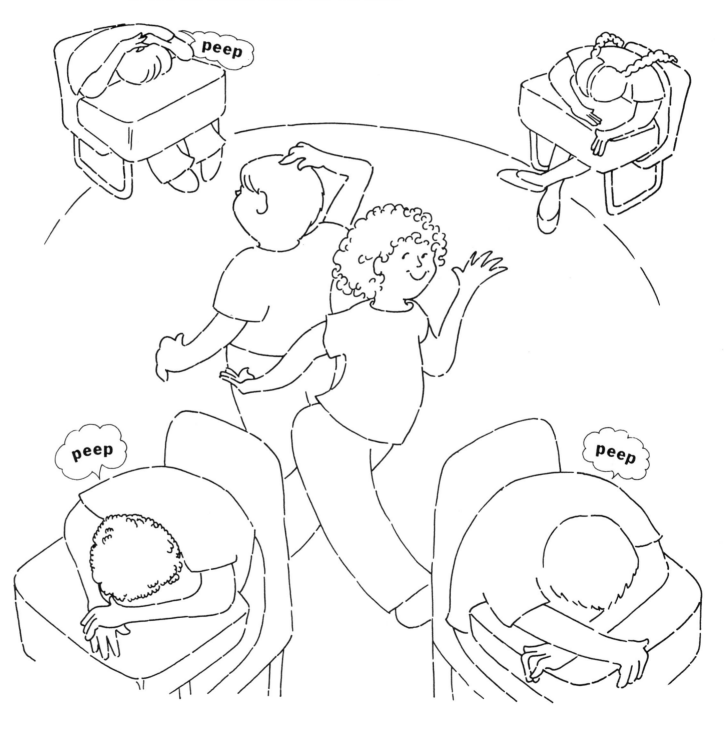

Poetry Time

Select a poem and read it to your class several times before using it for a lesson. Children need to become familiar with it before having to perform a task.

★ Read a poem to your class leaving out some words. Students must fill in the words you omit.

Mary had a little _____.
It's fleece was _____ as snow.

★ Children listen to a poem. They draw a picture to show what is happening.

Whiskey Friskey
Hippity hop.
Up he runs
To the treetop.

★ Children listen as you read a short verse with lines reversed. They repeat the verse in the correct order.

Little Miss Muffet
Sat on a tuffet
Along came a spider
Eating her curds and whey.

Rhyme Time

You will need to do a lot of oral practice with children to help them hear rhyming words. Reproduce the cards on pages 111 - 114. Color them, cut them apart, and laminate them. Begin with a few cards, building up to the full set as children become better able to hear the rhyming sounds.

Work with a small group in the beginning.

1. Show each of the cards you will be using to your students. Ask them to name the object. If your students cannot name it, say the name clearly for them and ask them to repeat it several times.

2. Give each child a card. Have one child at a time lay his/her card on the table. The child says the name of the picture. The teacher then holds up one card at a time. Everyone says the name of that card and the name of the card on the table. If they rhyme, the teacher lays the card down next to it. If they do not rhyme, the teacher holds up another card and the process is repeated. Keep the number of cards limited in the beginning.

3. When everyone in the group has a rhyming match for his/her card, go around the group and have each child show the two cards and say the rhyming words.

4. As children become more familiar with rhyming words, you can challenge them to come up with another word that rhymes with their pair.

         Readiness Fundamentals

Note: Reproduce these patterns to use with the activity on page 110.

Readiness Fundamentals

Note: Reproduce these patterns to use with the activity on page 110.

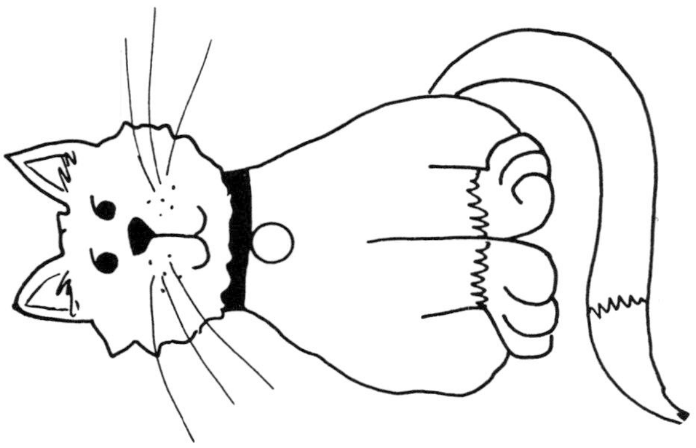

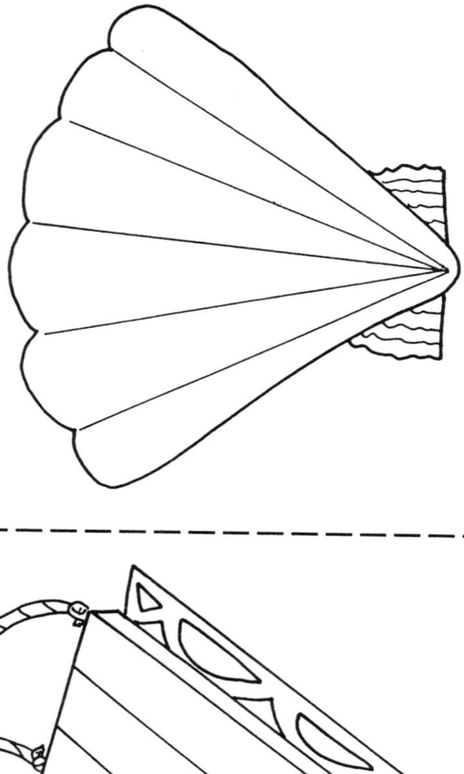

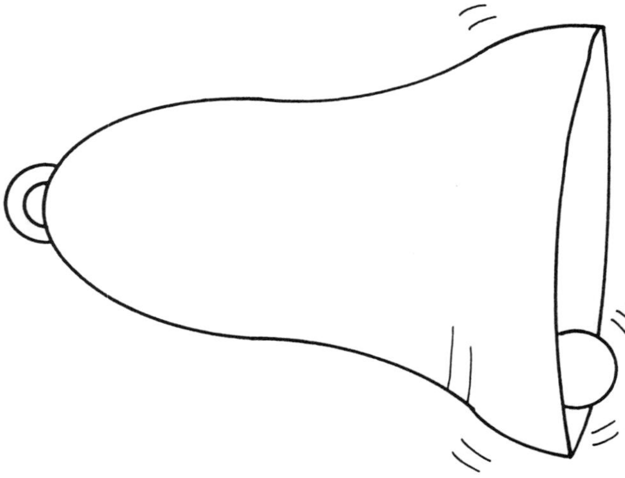

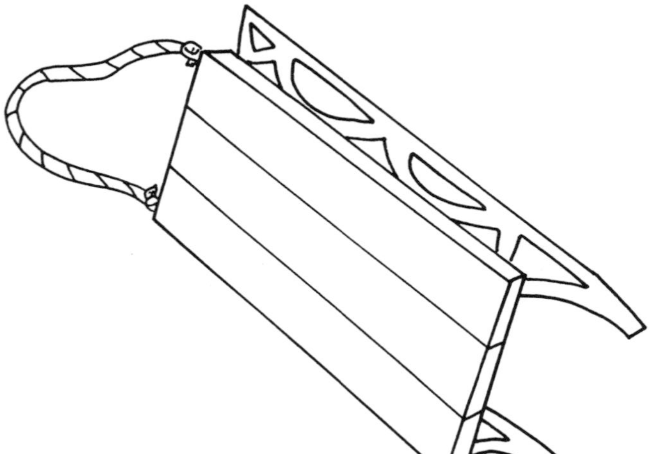

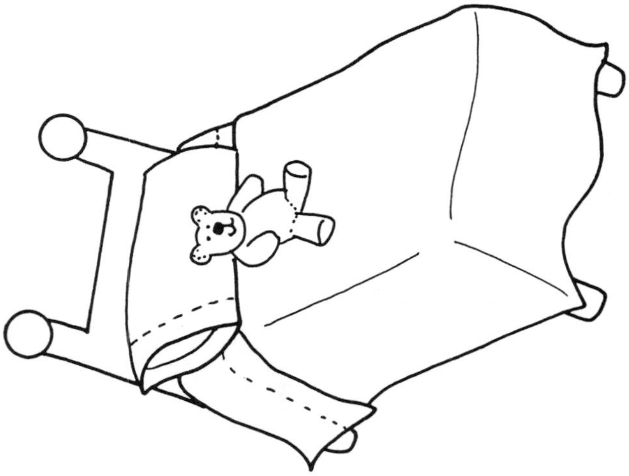

Readiness Fundamentals

Note: Reproduce these patterns to use with the activity on page 110.

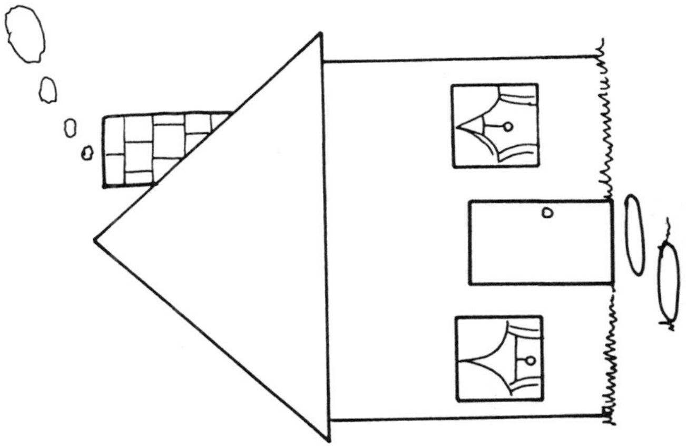

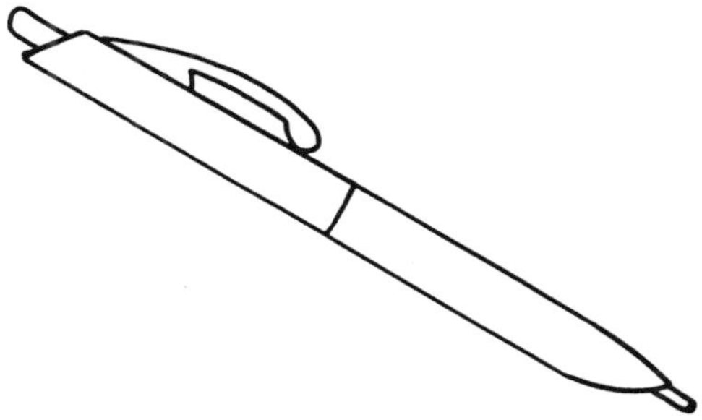

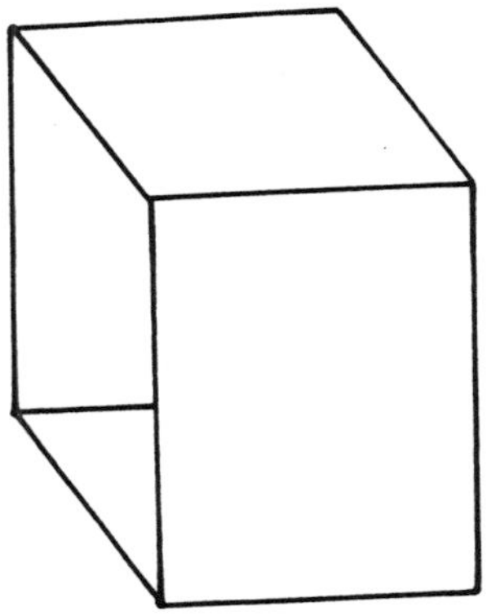

Note: Reproduce these patterns to use with the activity on page 110.

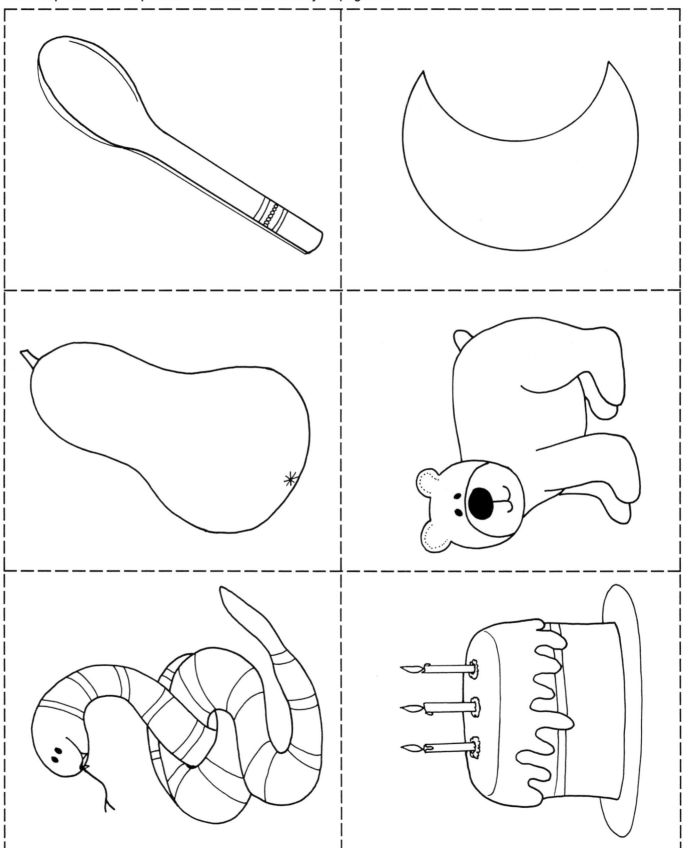

Readiness Fundamentals

Story Time

Select books that are appropriate to your students age and interests. Begin with stories containing few characters and events, moving up to more complicated ones as your students become better listeners.

1. Read a short story to the class. They have to name all the characters when you are finished. More able or mature students can be asked to give a word describing each character.
   "The story is about a cat and a mouse."
   "The baby bear has brown fuzzy hair and cries a lot."

2. Set a task before you read the story to the children. The children must listen carefully to find the answer.
   "What three things did Max have to find?"
   "What did the princess forget?"

3. Read a very familiar story deliberately making mistakes. Children are to correct the mistakes as they hear them.
   "Once upon a time there were two Billy Goats Gruff."

4. Give students specific words to listen for and a signal to give when they hear that word.
   "Every time you hear a color word raise your hand."

Read favorite stories to your children more than once. It is comforting to hear familiar tales where you can anticipate the humorous or exciting parts. Also children will get something new out of the story each time they hear it.

 Readiness Fundamentals

Riddles

Answering riddles requires careful listening to all elements being spoken. If the riddle asks, "What is round, red on the outside, white on the inside, and tastes good?" and the child answers "ball" or "orange", you know that only part of the clues were heard. When a child gets the correct answer, ask, "How did you know it was an apple?"

Younger students may need picture as well as oral clues. For those children, reproduce the picture cards on pages 117 and 118. Cut them apart, glue to tag, and laminate. Set the cards on the chalk tray. Read the riddles one at a time. Have children find the correct pictures.

I am white and fluffy. I have long ears. My tail is like a cotton puff. I like to eat carrots. (rabbit)

I am on your face. You use me to smell with. What am I? (nose)

I can be round or square. There are numbers on my face. My hands tell you what time it is. (clock)

I have a long neck and legs. I can reach the top of trees to eat the leaves. What am I? (giraffe)

I live in the water. I have fins and a tail to help me swim. I breathe with gills. What am I? (fish)

I am long and thin. I have a point at one end and an eraser at the other end. You can write with me. What am I? (pencil)

I am a person. I work at school. I help you learn. Who am I? (teacher)

I am big and yellow. I have many windows. I carry children to school. What am I? (bus)

Note: Reproduce these cards to use with the riddle activity on the preceding page.

Note: Reproduce these cards to use with the riddle activity on the preceding page.

Following Oral Directions
Activity Sheets

The activities on page 120 through 143 require children to use crayons, pencils, and/or scissors as they follow oral directions.

In order to make the activities accessible to children not yet ready to do "paper-pencil" type tasks, each teacher direction page contains a variation on the activity which provides practice in the same listening skills, but is done using cards, flannel board pieces, etc.

       Readiness Fundamentals

Circles

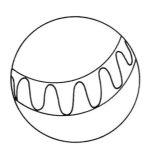  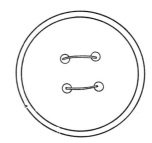

Oral Directions for Page 121

• Reproduce the page for each child doing the activity.
• Students will need a set of crayons.

1. Put a black X on the balloon.

2. Color the sun yellow.

3. Put a green line under the happy face.

4. Make a blue circle around the button.

5. Put an orange box around the clock.

6. Color the ball red.

Variation

This variation does not require children to mark the circles.

Reproduce page 121 several times.
Glue the page to a sheet of heavy construction paper or tag.
Cut out the circles. Put each set in an envelope.

Give an envelope to each child doing the activity.
The child takes out the circles. You give an oral direction which
the child follows by placing the circles on his/her work area.

1. Show me the _____.

2. Put the ball on your table.
   Put the sun over the ball.
   Put the balloon under the ball.

3. Put these in a row: first the button,
   next the sun, last the smiling face.

Continue giving directions as an appropriate level of difficulty for your students.

Circles

121

Shapes

   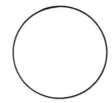 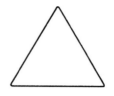

Oral Directions for Page 123

Reproduce the page for each child doing the activity. They will also need a set of crayons. Review the names of the different shapes before children coloring them.

1. Color the big circle blue.

2. Color the small triangle orange.

3. Color the small square purple.

4. Color the big triangle green.

5. Color the small circle red.

6. Color the big square yellow.

7. Put a black X on all of the big shapes.

8. Put a black circle around all of the small shapes.

Variation

This variation does not require children to mark the circles. Make a set of large and small circles, squares, and triangles out of felt to use on a flannel board.

Go through the pieces naming each one before you begin. Have children select and place pieces according to your directions.

1. Put all of the large shapes on the flannel board.

2. Find all of the small shapes and put them on the board.

3. Put the big triangle on the board. Now put the small triangle above it.

4. Put the big circle on the board. Put the small circle inside the big circle.

Continue giving directions as an appropriate level of difficulty for your students.

 Readiness Fundamentals

Shapes

Readiness Fundamentals

Quack, Baa, Hiss

Oral Directions for Page 125

Reproduce the page for each child doing the activity. They will also need a set of crayons. Review the names of the different animals and practice the sounds they make before children begin the lesson.

1. Take your orange crayon.
   Color the animal that says "Meow."

2. Take your red crayon.
   Color the animal that says "Oink."

3. Take your brown crayon.
   Color the animal that says "Woof."

4. Take your black crayon.
   Color the animal that says "Baa."

5. Take your yellow crayon.
   Color the animal that says "Quack."

6. Take your green crayon.
   Color the animal that says "Hiss."

Variation

This variation does not require children to color the animals.

Find pictures of a pig, dog, duck, sheep, snake, and cat. Or enlarge the animal pictures on page 125, cut them out and mount on tag. Show each picture to your students and ask them to make the sound that the animal shown makes. Once they are familiar with each sound, place all of the cards on the chalk tray and give the following oral directions.

1. Find the animal that says _____.

2. Put the dog in front of the sheep.

3. Find the animals with four legs.

Continue giving directions as an appropriate level of difficulty for your students.

Quack, Baa, Hiss

Readiness Fundamentals

Down the Road We Go

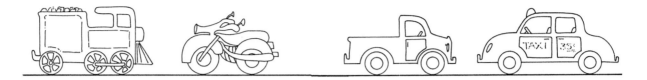

Oral Directions for Page 127

Reproduce the page for each child doing the activity. They will also need a set of crayons or a pencil. Review the names of the different vehicles and discuss their function before they begin the lesson.

1. Find the star.
   Put an X on the one a farmer can carry hay in.

2. Find the apple.
   Put an X on the one that helps put out fires.

3. Find the balloon.
   Put an X on the one that carries freight from city to city.

4. Find the sun.
   Put an X on the one your family can ride in.

5. Find the cat.
   Put an X on the one that carries children to school.

6. Find the smile.
   Put an X on the one with two big wheels.

Variation

Collect a variety of toy vehicles. Have children name each one and tell what it is used for. Then give oral directions such as these.

1. Find the one that your family can ride in.

2. Find the ones with more than four wheels.

3. Find the one that can fly through the air.

Continue giving directions as an appropriate level of difficultly for your students.

Down the Road

Readiness Fundamentals

Make a Clown

Oral Directions for Page 129

Reproduce the page for each child doing the activity. They will also need a set of crayons. Discuss what a clown does and what his/her face might look like. Show pictures of clown faces if you have them available. If not, draw some simple ones on the chalkboard as you discuss what the eyes, ear, nose, etc. might look like.

1. Trace the big circle on your paper.

2. Draw a nose for the clown.

3. Make a line for the mouth under the nose.

4. Make two eyes for the clown.

5. Draw a hat on top of his head.

6. Add some red hair.

Variation

Reproduce the clown face shape on page 129 and the clown face "parts" on pages 130-131. Use these as patterns for cutting out shapes to use on a flannel board. Color the pictures, cut them out and glue a Velcro dot to the back of each so they will stick to the flannel board.

Put the face piece on the flannel board, then give oral directions for completing a face.

1. Put a nose in the middle of the face.

2. Put a little mouth under the nose.

3. Put the tall hat on the clown.

Continue giving directions until the face is complete. Give additional directions to create a different face.

Make a Clown

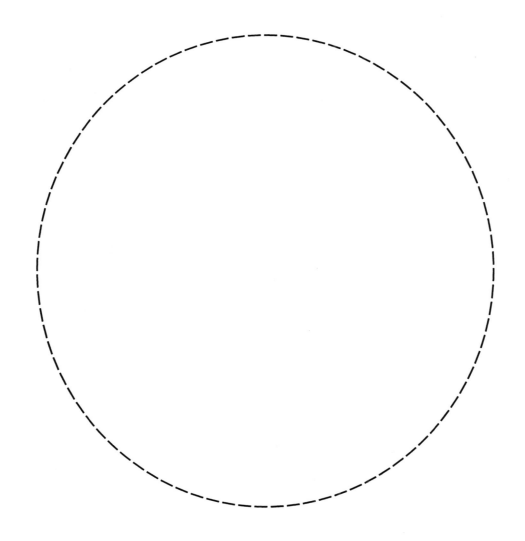

129

Readiness Fundamentals

Note: Reproduce these patterns to use with the flannel board activity on page 128.

ears

hats

hair

Note: Reproduce these patterns to use with the flannel board activity on page 128.

Clown Patterns

noses

mouth shapes

collars

eyes

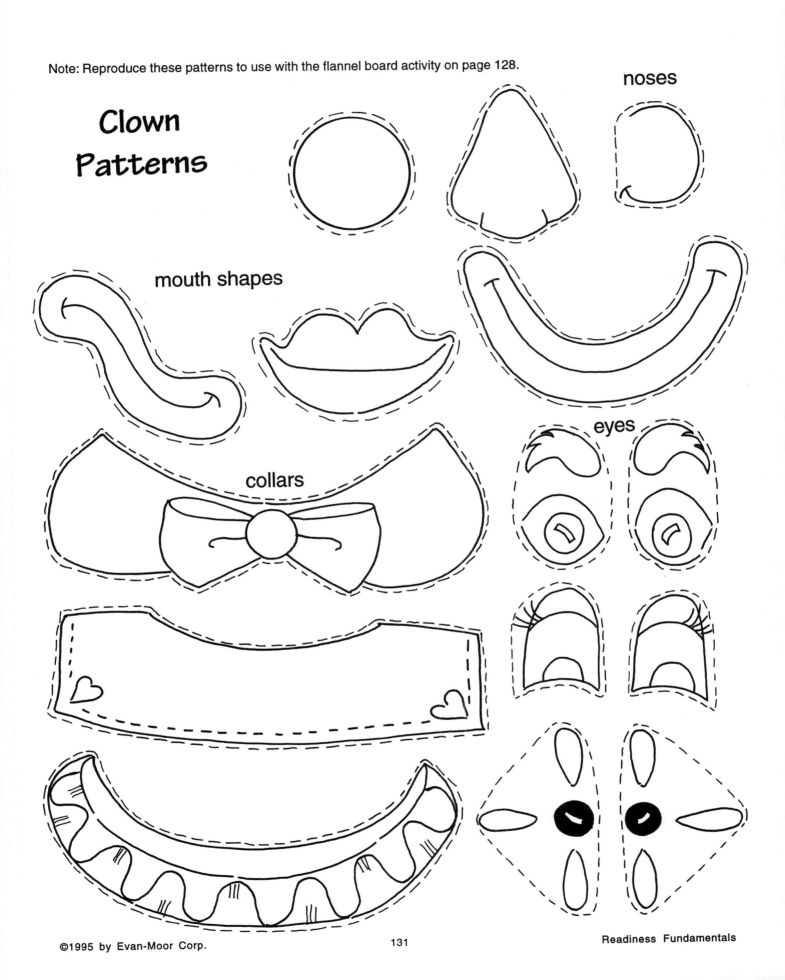

Readiness Fundamentals

Toy Box

Oral Directions for Page 133

Reproduce the page for each child doing the activity. They will also need a set of crayons or a pencil. Have the children name each of the toys and describe how it can be used before beginning the activity sheet.

1. Put a line under the toy you use to build things.

2. Color the toy that bounces green.

3. Put a circle around all the toys with wheels.

4. Put a dot on the toys that go up in the air.

5. Color the toy that is an animal.

6. Put a black X on the toys you have at home.

Variation

Collect a variety of toys. Have children identify the toys by name and use. Give oral directions for children to follow using these toys.

1. Find a toy with wheels. Put it on the table.

2. Show me all of the toys that are animals.

3. Put the smallest toy next to the tallest toy.

Continue giving directions as an appropriate level of difficultly for your students.

Toy Box

133

Listen and Draw

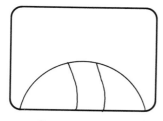 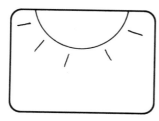 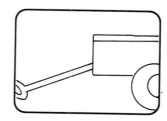 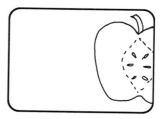

Oral Directions for Page 135

Reproduce the page for each child doing the activity. They will also need a set of crayons or a pencil. Children listen to the riddle, then draw the answer in the correct box.

1. I am round.
I am made of rubber.
I bounce.
You can throw me.

2. I am up in the sky.
I shine a bright light.
I make the day warm.
You cannot see me at night.

3. I have four wheels.
I have a handle.
You can pull your toys around in me.

4. I am red on the outside and white on the inside.
I have seeds in the middle.
I am a fruit.
I taste good.

Variation

Have a collection of real objects in class. Tell a riddle describing the object by shape, size, color, use, etc. Children have to find the correct object, bring it to the teacher, and give its name.

The collection should contain objects with which you wish the children to become more familiar. For example: toys, tools used at school, pieces of clothing, etc.

Listen and Draw

1

2

3

4

What Do I Have On?

Oral Directions for Page 137

Reproduce the page for each child doing the activity. They will also need a set of crayons. Have children name the pieces of clothing and discuss when they would be worn before beginning the lesson.

1. Color what you can sleep in blue.

2. Color the exercise clothes purple.

3. Color what you wear on your feet black.

4. Color what you wear on your hands orange.

5. Color what you could wear on a rainy day yellow.

6. Color what you wear to go swimming red.

Variation

Bring a box of clothing of various kinds into the classroom. Have children name the items. Give oral directions about the clothing having them either select the item and bring it to you, put items into categories you name, or put the clothing on following your directions. For example:

1. Find everything you wear on your feet. Now put the socks in one pile and the shoes in another pile.

2. Find a hat and put it on your head.

3. Put on the clothes you would wear outside on a rainy day.

Continue giving directions as an appropriate level of difficulty for your students.

What Do I Have On?

Readiness Fundamentals

Fish Bowl

Directions for Page 139

Reproduce the page for each child doing the activity. They will also need a set of crayons. Talk about what might be in the fish bowl before you begin.

1. Trace the fish bowl.

2. Draw two orange fish in the fish bowl.

3. Make a green plant in the fish bowl.

4. Draw some black rocks at the bottom of the bowl.

5. Color some blue water in the bowl for your fish.

6. Color the table brown.

Variation

Cut out the following items from felt:

          a fish bowl shape
          several small fish
          a green plant
          some rock shapes

Place the fish bowl on a flannel board. Give directions about the placement of the fish, plant, and rocks in the bowl. Children listen to your directions and move the pieces around.

Continue giving directions as an appropriate level of difficultly for your students.

Fish Bowl

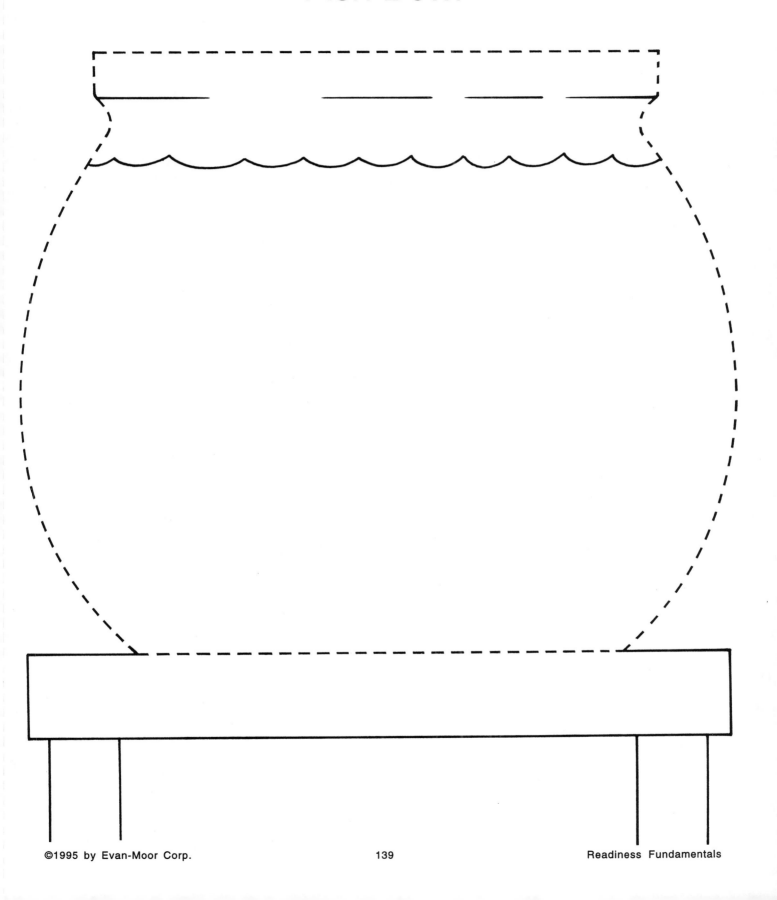

139

Fruit Salad

Directions for Page 141

Reproduce the page for each child doing the activity. They will also need a set of crayons. Have children point to and name all of the types of fruit on the page before you begin giving directions.

1. Find the star. Color the apple red.

2. Find the X. Color the pear green.

3. Find the balloon. Color the cherry red.

4. Find the sun. Color the orange orange.

5. Find the cat. Color the banana yellow.

6. Find the box. Color the grapes purple.

Variation

Have a collection of real fruits. Have children name each kind. Tell a riddle describing one of the fruits by shape, color, size, or other characteristic. Children have to find the correct fruit, bring it to the teacher, and give its name.

When you are finished use the fruit for a tasting experience so children can experience the taste of different varieties.

You can do the same activity with types of vegetables also.

Fruit Salad

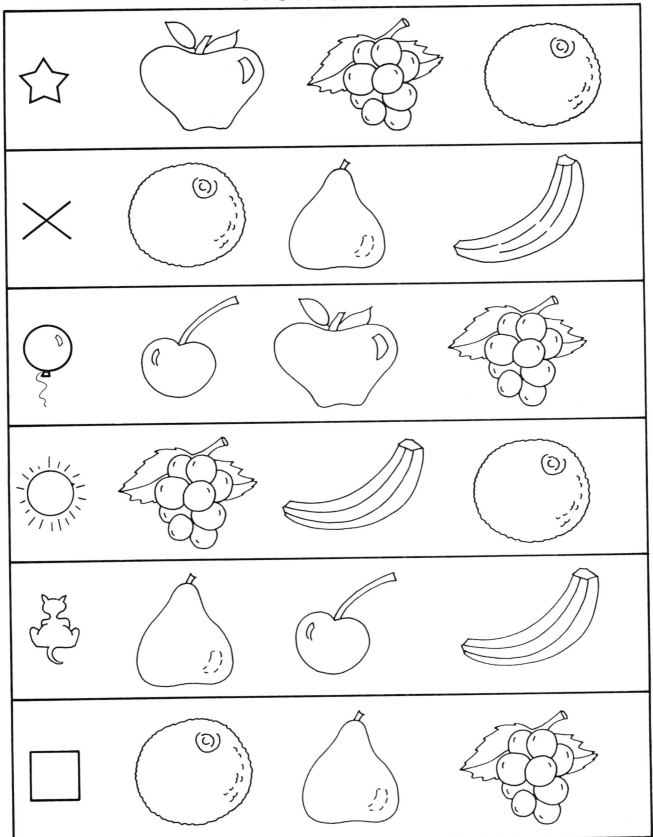

The Circus Parade

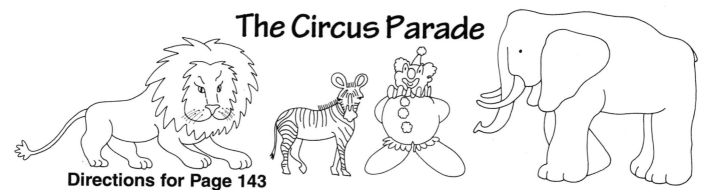

Directions for Page 143

Reproduce the page for each child doing the activity. They will also need a set of crayons. Have children point to and name all of the animals and circus people represented on the page before you begin giving directions.

1. Put a red X on the biggest animal.

2. Put a blue line under the animal with stripes.

3. Put a green circle around the little clown.

4. Put a black X on the biggest clown.

5. Put a yellow line under the lion.

6. Put an orange circle around the acrobat.

Variation

Enlarge the pictures on your copy machine. Paste the pieces to cards made from heavy construction paper or tag. Color the pieces and laminate them.

Sets the cards in the chalk tray and give oral directions such as these.

1. "Put the tall clown in front of the small clown."
2. "Find the animal that has a long trunk."
3. "Put all of the animals together."
4. "Put all of the people together."
5. "Find the people who make us laugh. What are they called?"

Continue giving directions as an appropriate level of difficultly for your students.

     Readiness Fundamentals

The Circus Parade

Readiness Fundamentals

Folding Paper Practice

Children are frequently ask to fold paper in a variety of ways. This can be a problem for children who have trouble following visual clues. Take your students through these folding practices giving oral as well as visual clues. Say what you are doing as you show what is to be done.

Two Boxes

"Hold your paper in two hands like this.

Fold this edge all the way over to the other edge.

Lay your paper down and rub it flat.

Open your paper and count the boxes you made.

One, two. Good work."

Four Boxes

(Repeat above.)

"Turn your paper like this.

Hold it in two hands like this.

Fold this edge all the way over to the other edge.

Lay your paper down and rub it flat."

Open your paper and count the boxes you made.

Listen and Follow Directions

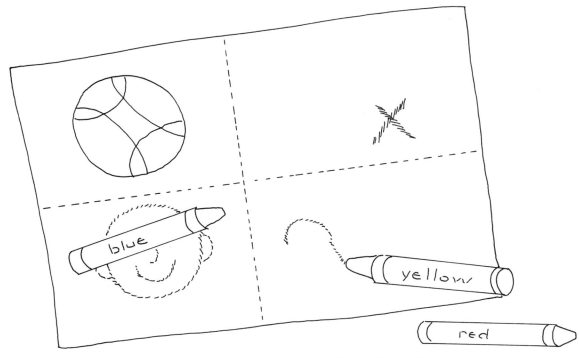

Have children follow the directions on page 144 to fold a piece of paper into four boxes.

Draw a picture of the boxes on the chalkboard. Point to the correct box as you give each directions.

Here are some samples of the directions you might give.

- Make a blue ball in the first box on your paper.

- Make two red lines in the last box on your paper.

- Make a little black X in the second box.

- Put a yellow circle around the black X.

- Make a happy face in the third box.

- Put an orange line over the blue ball.

- Put a purple hat on the happy face.

- Draw a surprise on the back of your paper.

145

Make an Origami Dog

Each child will need a 9" x 9" (23 x 23 cm) sheet of paper. White or light brown paper is the most versatile. You will need to demonstrate the steps as you give oral directions to your students.

1. "Put your paper in front of you on your desk. Lay it so it looks like a diamond."

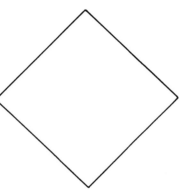

2. "Fold the paper so that the top point matches the bottom point. Rub the fold so your paper is smooth and flat."

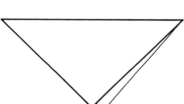

3. "Now your paper looks like a triangle. Take the point on the right side and fold it down a little to make an ear for your dog. Make an ear on the left side too."

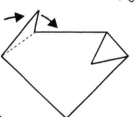

4. "Look at the bottom point. Fold the paper up to make the dog's nose and mouth."

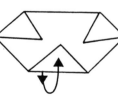

5. "Take a crayon and make eyes and a nose for your dog."

6. "Color your dog. Can you think of a good name for your dog.?"

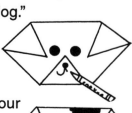

146   Readiness Fundamentals

Visual Perception Skills

Section four provides activities to help children improve their gross and fine visual perception skills. The activities help develop the ability to:

- recognize objects by appearance
- relate pictures and models to real places and things
- notice and describe likenesses and differences
- recognize and build patterns
- sort and match
- compare
- put things in a logical order
- put things together and take them apart
- observe things from different spatial viewpoints
- locate things around the classroom, school and neighborhood
- copy what the teacher does
- begin to recognize letters and numbers

Reading, writing, and math all become difficult for the child with visual perception problems. Observe your students and they do the activities in this book. If you find someone who has more than a little difficulty or continues to have difficulty over a long period, take a closer look. The earlier we identify problems such as dyslexia, the sooner we can offer these children help.

Describe it

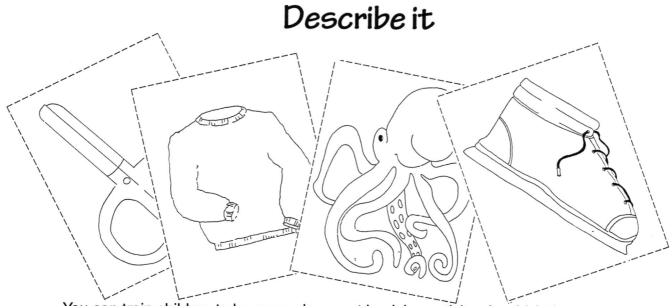

You can train children to be more observant by doing activites in which they must look carefully and then describe what they have seen. Discuss the various ways objects can be described:

color

size

shape

use

material it is made of

taste

location

Alike and Different

Show children two objects that are similar in two or more ways. They are to describe how the objects are alike and how they are different.

- a slice of brown bread and a graham cracker
- a round cookie and a rice cracker
- a quarter and a dime
- a flag and a handkerchief
- a clock and a wristwatch

Using Picture Cards

(page 149-150)

Reproduce the picture cards on the following pages. Cut the cards apart to use with the following activities.

1. Give a child a card to describe. Display hat card and two or three others to another child. That child must try to select the card that was described.

2. Place several cards on the table in a row. Discuss the order of the cards with students. Mix the cards up and select a child to put them back in order.

Note: Reproduce these cards to use with the activity on page 148. Color, cut-out, and laminate before use.

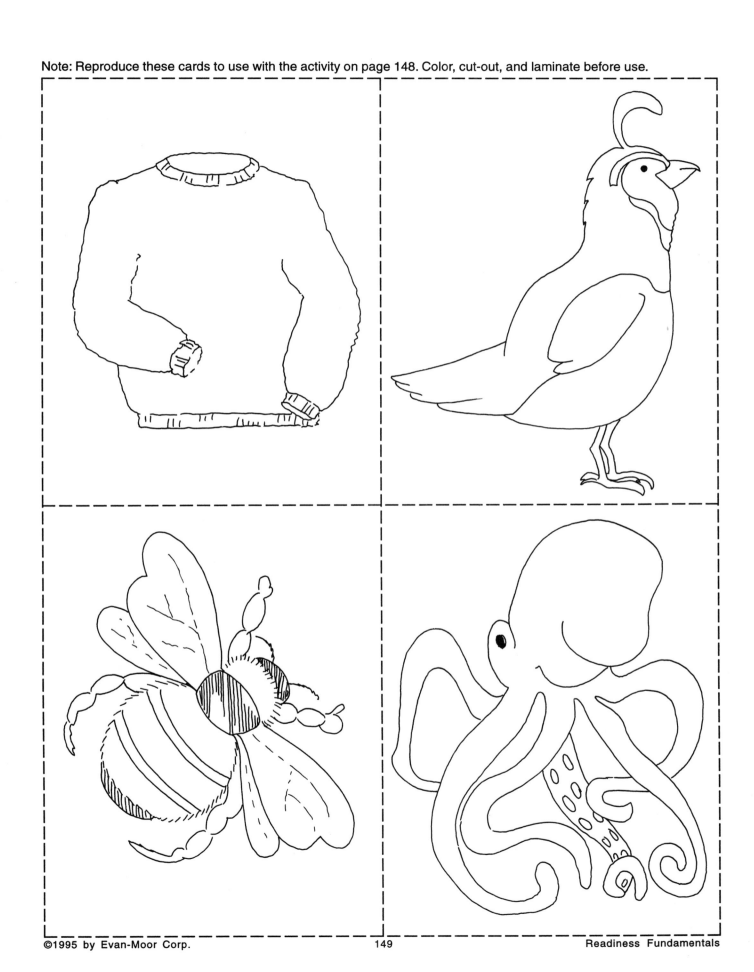

Note: Reproduce these cards to use with the activity on page 148. Color, cut-out, and laminate before use.

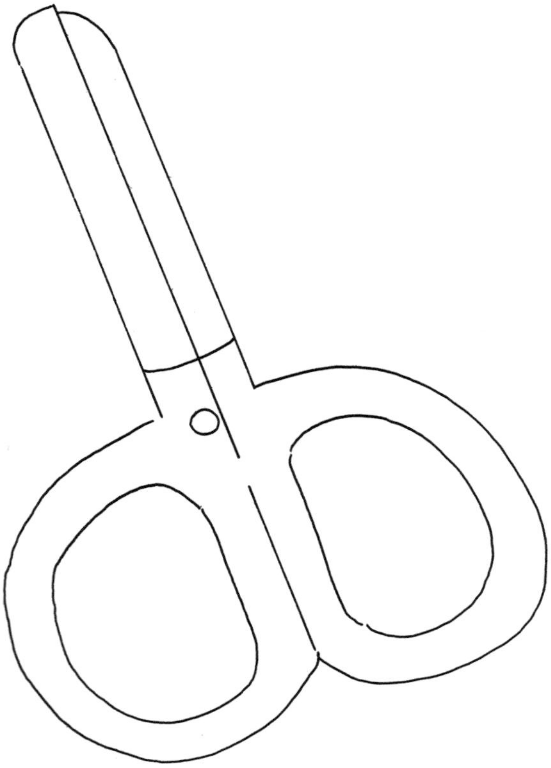

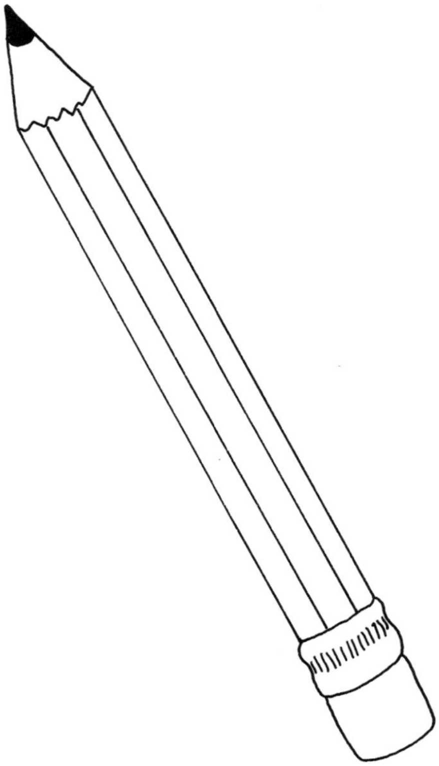

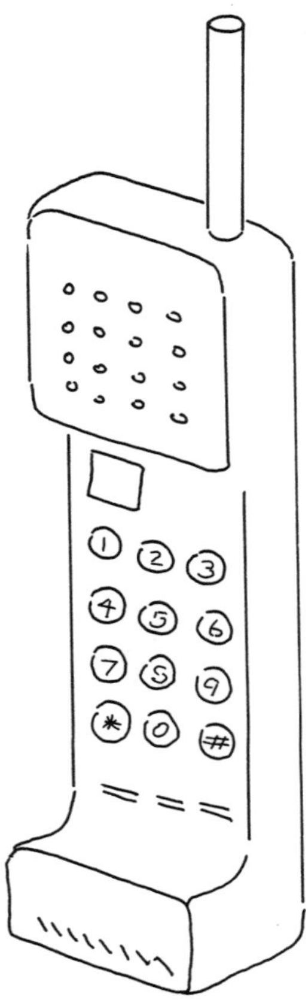

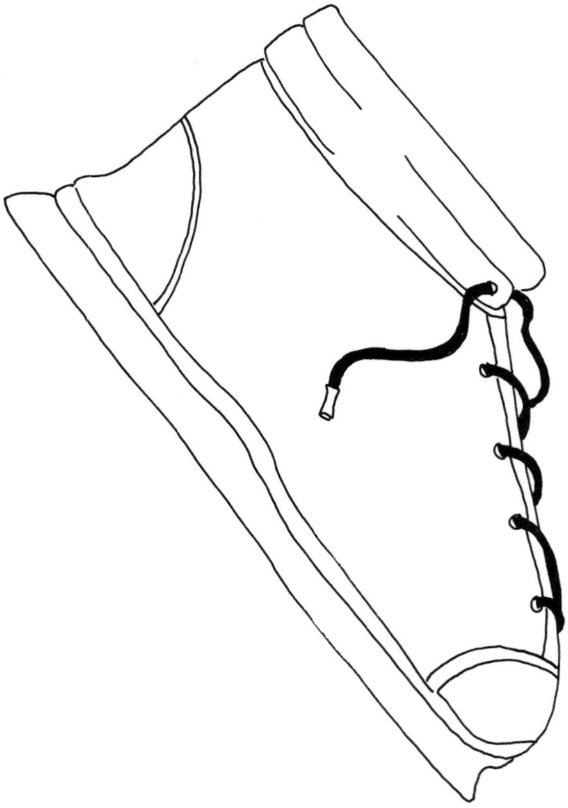

Note: Reproduce these cards to use with the activity on page 148. Color, cut-out, and laminate before use.

Who Is It?

Who Am I Thinking About?

Have three children come to the front of the classroom. The rest of the children close their eyes. The teacher describes one of the thre children standing in front of the room. The other children open their eyes and try to decide which child was described.

Variations

• The teacher or a student describes someone in the classroom. The other students try to decide who it is.
• Describe someone in the school who is not present in the room.
• Describe someone from a favorite story.

Find the Picture

Find a picture in a magazine that contains three or more people. Select someone to describe one person in the picture. The other players try to guess who has been described.

Variation

Have children draw pictures of someone (real or fictional) to use in playing the game. Put the pictues on a bulletin board for everyone to see. Select a child to describe a picture. The other players try to find the picture.

                                       Readiness Fundamentals

What is Missing?

There is nothing to make for this game. Just collect several small items from around the classroom. Begin with as few as three items, building up to a larger number as children become able to remember a larger number of items.

1. Have the players sit where they can see the items clearly.
2. Name all the items for your students. Give them a minute to study the items.
3. Have them close their eyes while you remove one item.
4. Players open their eyes and try to decide what item was removed.

Repeat the game several times, increasing the number of items if your students seem ready.

Variations
Include items that are the same except for color or size (a big blue button, a small white button, and a button with flower on it). This requires the children to describe the items as well as name them.

If you are working with more than three items, remove two items at the same time. This makes it harder to remember.

         Readiness Fundamentals

The Order of Things

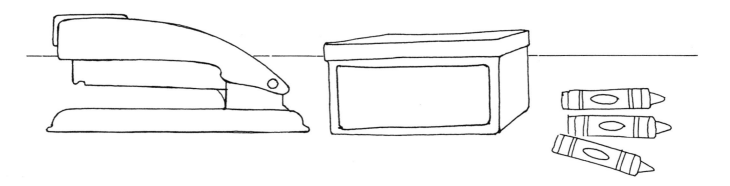

Collect several small items from around the classroom (stuffed animals are fun). Begin with only a few items. The more objects you use the harder the task. Add more as children become able to remember a larger number of items.

1. Place three or more items in a row.
2. Have the players sit where they can see the items clearly.
3. Name all the items for your students. Give them a minute to study the items.
4. Have them close their eyes while you make a change.
5. Players open their eyes and try to put everything back into its original order.

Repeat the game several times, increasing the number of changes if your students seem ready.

Patterns

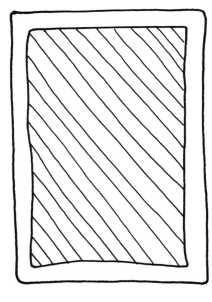 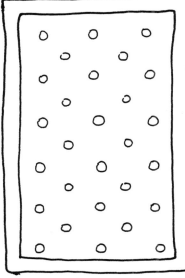 

Patterning provides visual and motor practice for your students. You will need to help them understand that to be a pattern, something must be repeated over and over again. Help children to see patterns in their environment and to verbalize them. Place to find patterns might include:

- clothing - look for stripes or patterns
- calendar - use cut-out shapes to mark the days building a pattern (Sept. 1 apple, Sept. 2 leaf, Sept. 3 apple, etc.)
- pictures - place pattern pictures all around the room for students to find
- people patterns - form lines of children in various patterns
- chairs - arrange chairs to form patterns (pushed in, pulled out)
- flowers, trees, etc. - these are often planted in patterns especially in gardens
- walkways and sidewalks
- fences
- patterns on buildings (bricks, wood slats, tile, etc.)

Build a Pattern

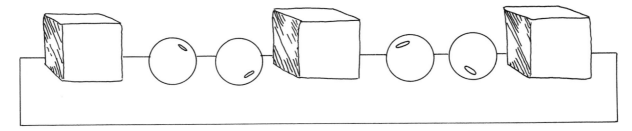

You should guide your students from simple patterns (a, b) to more complex ones (abb,aba, abc, etc.). It helps many children to have them verbalize the pattern they are examining as they touch it.

Objects for Patterning

There are many items around the classroom, the playground, and from home that can be used for patterning practice. Be sure to consider the maturity and age of your students in choosing items for them to use in patterning. The younger the child, the bigger the items must be for safety.

- large beads and shoe laces
- colored macaroni pieces
- shape blocks
- small toys
- shapes cut from paper
- rubber stamps and stamp pads
- leaves
- shells and rocks
- spoons of different sizes
- cereal pieces
- jar lids of various types
- nuts and bolts

Levels of Patterning

1. Have children copy you as you model the pattern

2. Have children copy a pattern you have made.

3. Have children extend a pattern you have begun.

4. Have children create their own patterns.

A Pattern Activity

Reproduce the patterns on the bottom of this page from felt or Pellon in several colors to use with the patterning form on page 158.

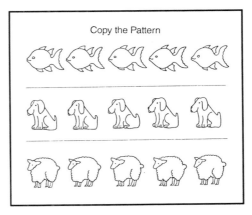

Copy the Pattern

1. Reproduce a copy of page 158 for each child doing the activity.

2. Teacher shows a pattern using fish on the flannel board. Children copy the pattern on their worksheet by coloring the fish in row one to match the teacher's pattern.

3. Teacher shows a pattern using the dogs on the flannel board. Children copy the pattern by coloring the dogs in row two to match the teacher's pattern.

4. Teacher shows a pattern using the lambs on the flannel board. Children copy the pattern by coloring the lambs in row three to match the teacher's pattern.

Note: Reproduce this page to use with activity on page 157.

Copy the Pattern

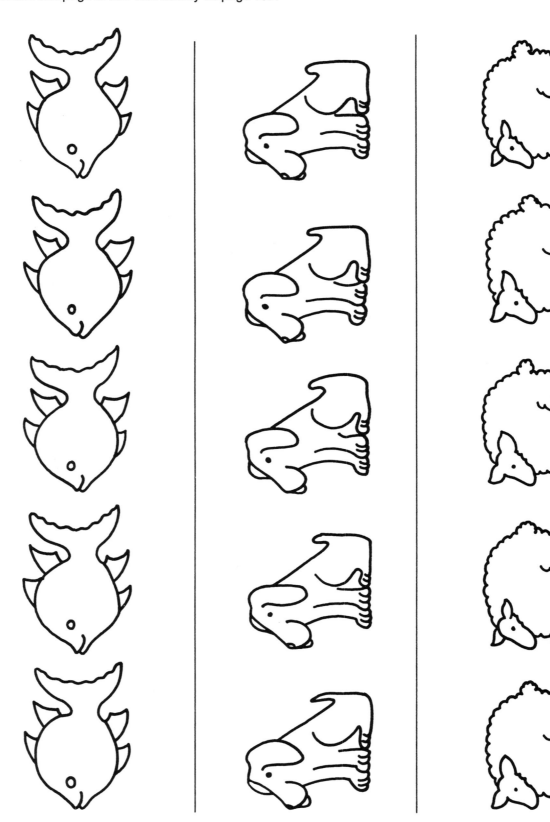

Readiness Fundamentals

Let's Play a Game

Do As I Do

The teacher or a student is the leader. Everyone else copies the motions demonstrated. Start with one or two easy movements. Gradually add a greater number and/or more difficult motions as students become better able to follow.

- Touch different parts of your body.
- Put your hands over your head, behind your back, in front of your body, etc.
- Swing your arms in opposition.
- Act out an activity such as washing a window, eating a banana, or making a sandwich.
- Hop around in a small circle on one foot.

Charades

Select someone to demonstrate a motion. The other players must guess what the motion represents. Be sure that all the players understand that they are to act out something the class can recognize.

- sweep the floor
- do a dance
- paint a wall
- pour a drink
- take a bath

       Readiness Fundamentals

"I See"

Play this variation of "I Spy" in the classroom or sitting outside on the lawn. Remind children of all of the ways they can describe things (size, color, shape, smell, touch, etc.).

1. Practice describing what is seen giving a characteristic and having everyone in the group find something that fits it. Say "I see something <u>green</u>." Each child names something green they see (grass, tree leaves, green paper on the chalkboard, a green pencil, etc.). Repeat this activity giving a different type of characteristic each time. Accept all reasonable answers.

2. Model the process of giving several clues and have the children guess what you see. Be sure the object you are describing is within the childrens' line of sight. Remind children to listen to the whole riddle before they try to answer it.

> "I see something round.
> It is made of rubber. It can bounce. I can throw it." (ball)

> "I see something that is made of cloth.
> It has four sides. It has stars and stripes." (flag)

> "I see something that is alive. It sings a pretty song.
> It has feathers. It can fly." (bird)

3. Have children be the person giving the riddle. Remind them to start with "I See" and to not tell the name of the object as they give the clues.

Let's Take a "Looking" Walk

Take advantage of good weather to take a "looking walk to practice visual perception skills.

Choose a Location
- the school yard
- the neighborhood
- a local park
- a business area
- a zoo or animal shelter
- a beach, pond, lake or river area
- a museum or aquarium

Set a "Looking" Task
- look for people (working, playing)
- look for animals
- look for types of buildings
- lookg for signs
- look for types of vehicles
- look for objects of a certain color or shape
- look for plants

When you return to school, discuss what has been seen. You may also have children illustrate what they have seen.

On rainy or snowy days you can line up by the windows and look for specific items instead of going outside for a walk.

Find It

Have children locate things in the classroom. Begin with easily located objects and move to less obvious ones.

Real Objects

Become more specific about what must be found as you practice the activity.

1. Show a real object such as a chair and have children find any other chairs around the room.

2. Show a real object such as a white shirt and have children find other white shirts in the room.

3. Show a real object such as a chalkboard eraser and have children find other chalkboard erasers in the classroom.

4. Show a real object that would be more difficult to locate at first glance (maybe a specific book or toy) and have children find it.

Pictures

Once children are successful finding objects using a real object as an example, repeat the activity showing drawings or photographs of items. Begin again with the more easily found objects and work up to less obvious ones.

How are We Alike?

Use the children themselves to practice visual discrimination and build an awareness of likenesses among us all at the same time. You must use very obvious similarities in the beginning, especially with your youngest students. Let as many children come up to share as volunteer.

1. Call up two children that are similar in several ways (hair color, eye color, height, way they are dressed, etc.). Ask "What is the same about _____ and _____?"

2. After children have had an opportunity to give some answers, call up a third child who is different from the other two in several ways. Ask "How is _____ the same?" This requires more thought as the similarities are more subtle. If your students have difficulty, help by asking questions such as "How many arms do they all have?" ""Can they all move around?" "What do they all have on their feet?" "Do they all have to eat?"

3. Call up a group of at least six children and divide them into two sets. See if the class can decide why each set goes together (girls in one set, boys in the other; blonds in one group, brown hair in another; tall children in one group, short in another; children in blue in one group, children in green in another; etc.) Rearrange the same group several times, asking children to tell why the groups go together.

4. Call up one child. Ask "Who is like _____?" Select a child who responds "I am." and have that child come up and explain how he/she is like the original child.

> "I am like Harry. I have boots on."
>
> "I am like Harry. I have long hair too."
>
> "I am like Harry. My tooth is gone."

Draw What I Draw

Guided drawing is an enjoyable and successful way to help children practice visual perception skills. They must watch carefully to see what details to include in their pictures. Drawing also helps children develop greater small muscle control and improve their ability to follow auditory and visual directions.

Teacher may draw on the chalkboard or use an overhead projector. Provide children with large sheets of paper and either pencils or crayons and you are ready to begin.

Select simple forms to draw in the beginning.

Draw each picture one step at a time. Allow adequate time for children to copy each step.

When the basic picture has been completed, allow time for students to add something of their own to the drawing.

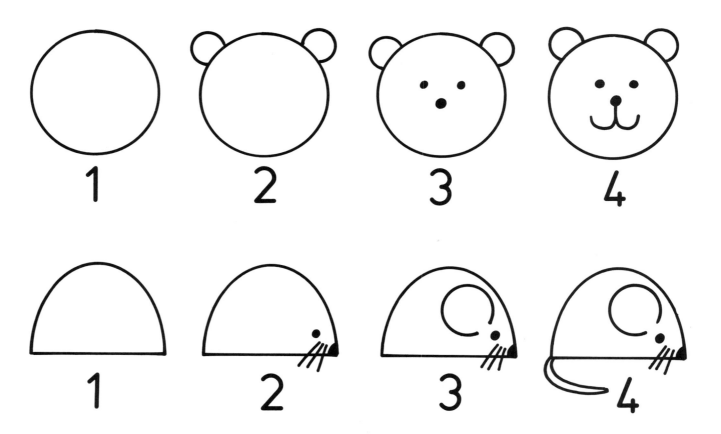

Visual Discrimination Activity Sheets
Pages 166 through 177

★ Pages 166 through 173 require children to look for at objects in a variety of ways. They have to find:
- objects which are the same
- objects which are different
- objects in silhouette form
- objects from a different viewpoint
- objects fitting in the same category
- objects hidden in a picture

The pages can be reproduced for children to complete using a crayon or pencil.

One or more copies may be made and put into plastic sleeves or laminated. Children use plastic counters and pieces of yarn to mark the correct answers to use for repeated practice in a center or with a small group of children having more difficulty.

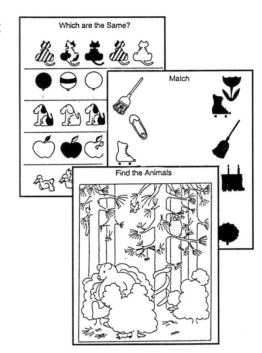

★ Page 174 asks children to cut out a "herd" of elephants and place them in order by size - largest to smallest.

★ Pages 175 through 177 require children to draw, either adding an element or completing a shape.

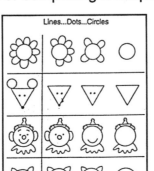
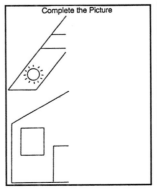

Readiness Fundamentals

Which are the Same?

Readiness Fundamentals

Which One is Different?

Match

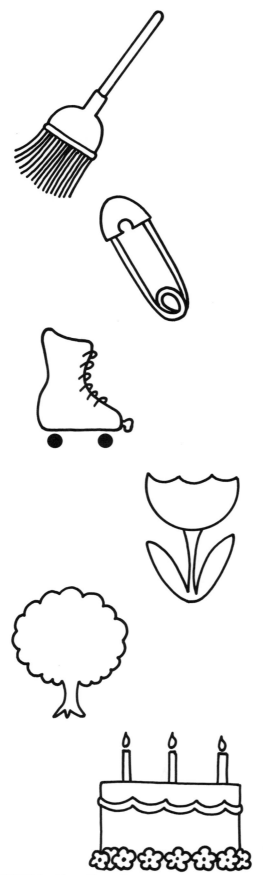

Readiness Fundamentals

Match

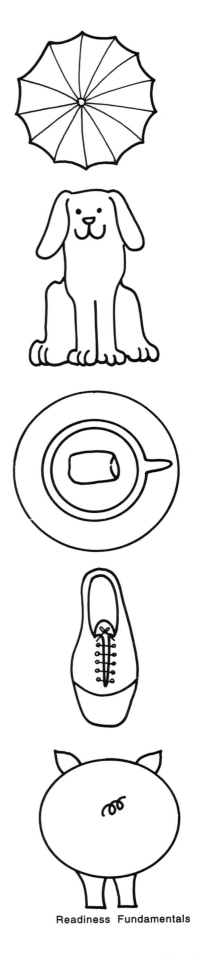

Teacher: Children are to mark the dog that is exactly like the one at the top of the page.

Dogs

170 Readiness Fundamentals

Teacher: Children are to mark the cat that is exactly like the one at the top of the page.

Cats

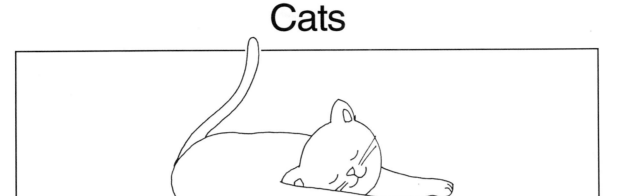

Find the Animals

172

Find the Toys

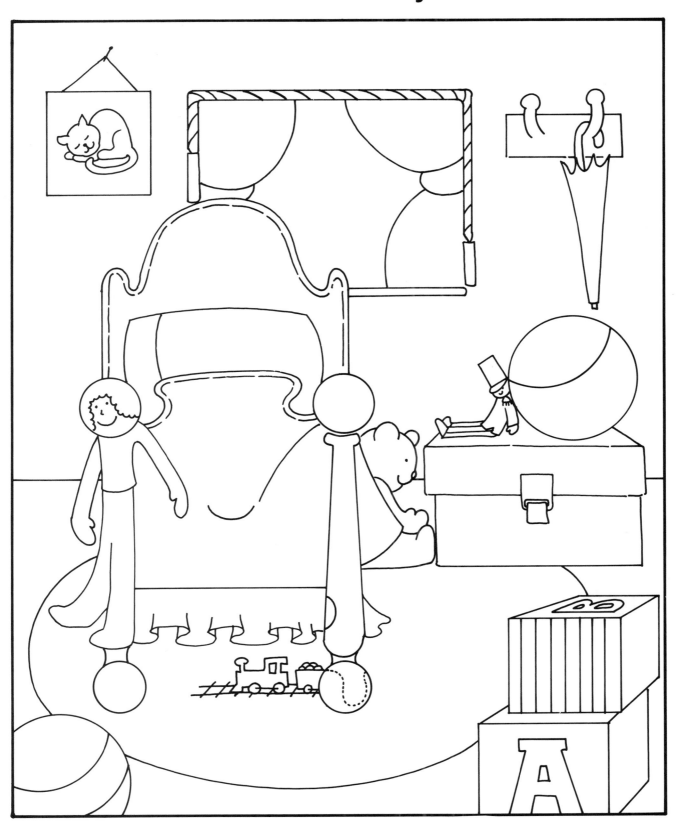

Teacher: Children are to paste the elephants in order from largest to smallest. Each child will need a 6" X 18" sheet of construction paper.

The Elephant Parade

Readiness Fundamentals

Teacher: Children are to make each picture in the row look like the first picture.

Lines...Dots...Circles

Complete the Picture

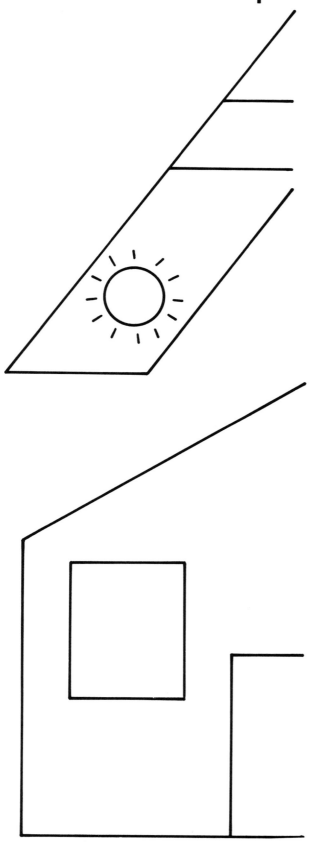

Complete the Picture

Jigsaw Puzzles

Jigsaw puzzles are wonderful for visual perception. You have the added benefit of working with small muscle control. Begin with puzzles having only a few sturdy pieces. Move up to more complicated ones as children become more proficient. Once your students can do a puzzle with 12 to 20 pieces you can often find suitable ones for very little money.

Making Your Own Puzzles

Often the jigsaw puzzles available with few pieces are expensive wooden ones. If you are unable to get such puzzles, try making your own. This way you can have a 2-4 piece puzzle which will be challenging enough at first for younger children.

1. Find an large, simple picture in a magazine.
2. Glue the picture to a piece of thin cardboard.
3. When the glue has dried, cut the puzzle into an appropriate number of pieces. An Exacto knife will probably work better than a pair of scissors.
4. Store the puzzle in an envelope or baggie.

Increase the number of pieces as students progress.

Pages 179 to 186 have paper puzzles of various types for your students to cut out and paste to another sheet of paper. These can also be used to make your own puzzles following the directions listed above.

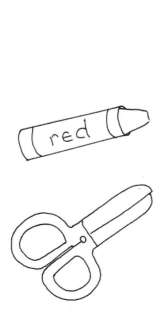

See the sailboat.

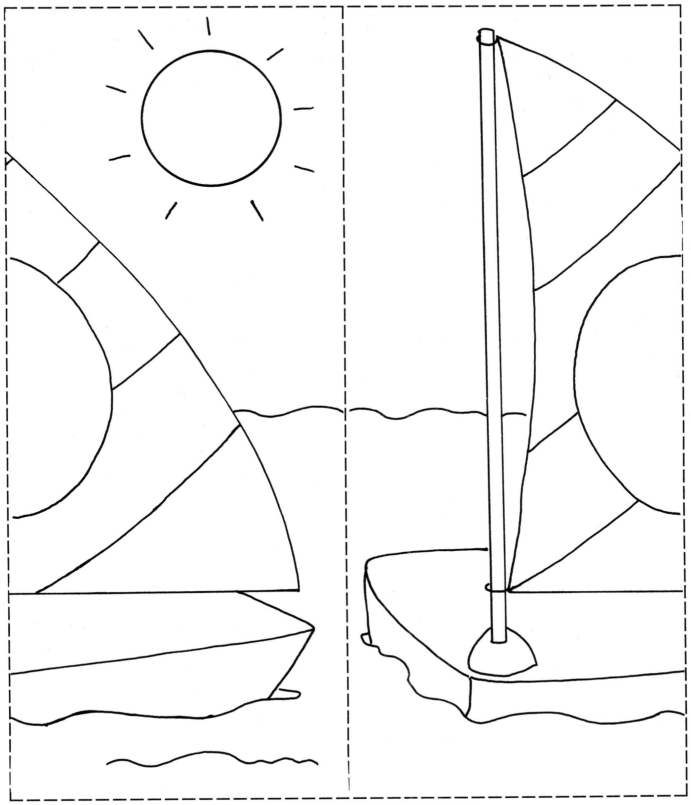

Readiness Fundamentals

School Bus

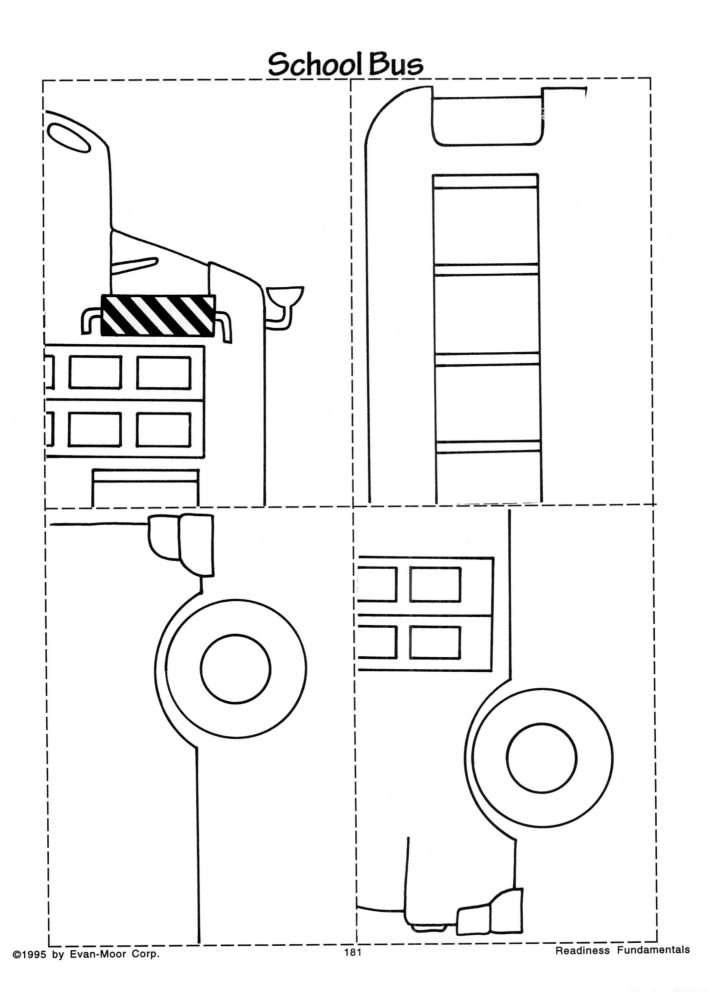

Readiness Fundamentals

Note: Each child will need this puzzle and a blank sheet of paper on which to paste it.

Note: Each child will need this puzzle and a blank sheet of paper on which to paste it.

 Readiness Fundamentals

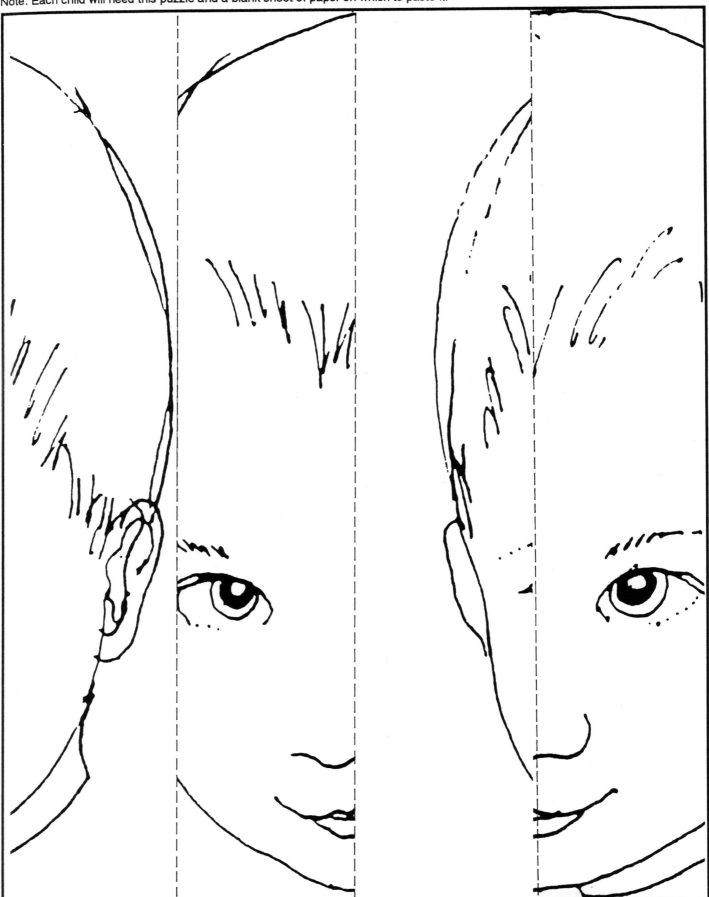

Readiness Fundamentals

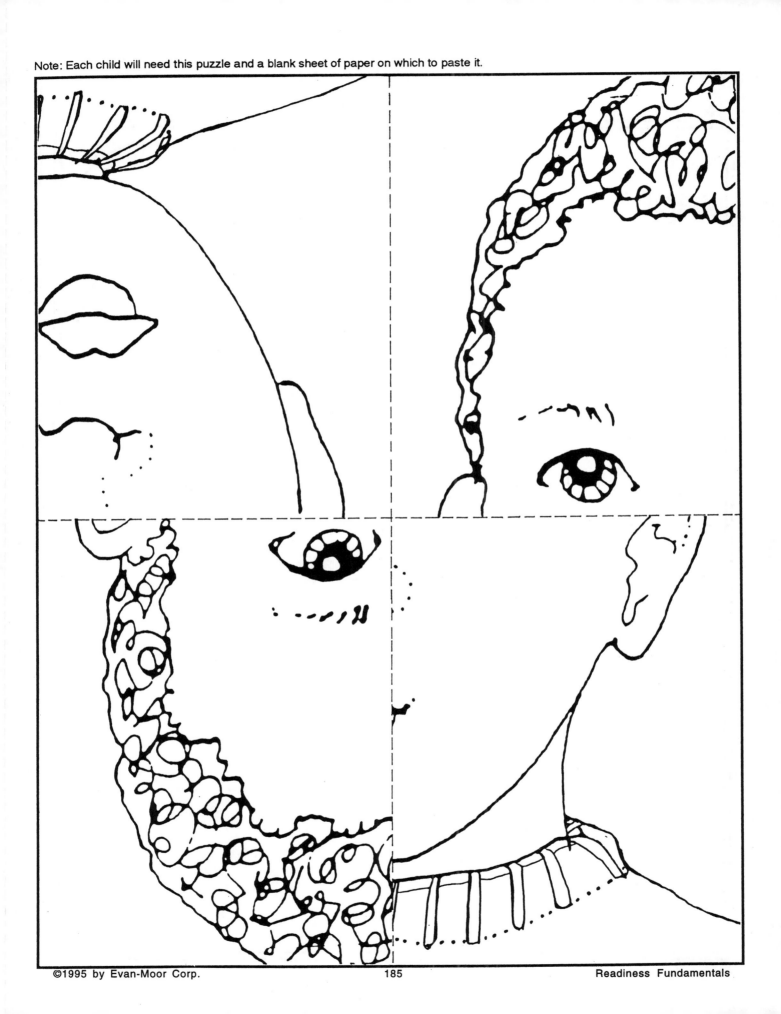

Teacher: Children are to paste the puzzle together on a 9" X 12" sheet of paper.

Dinosaur

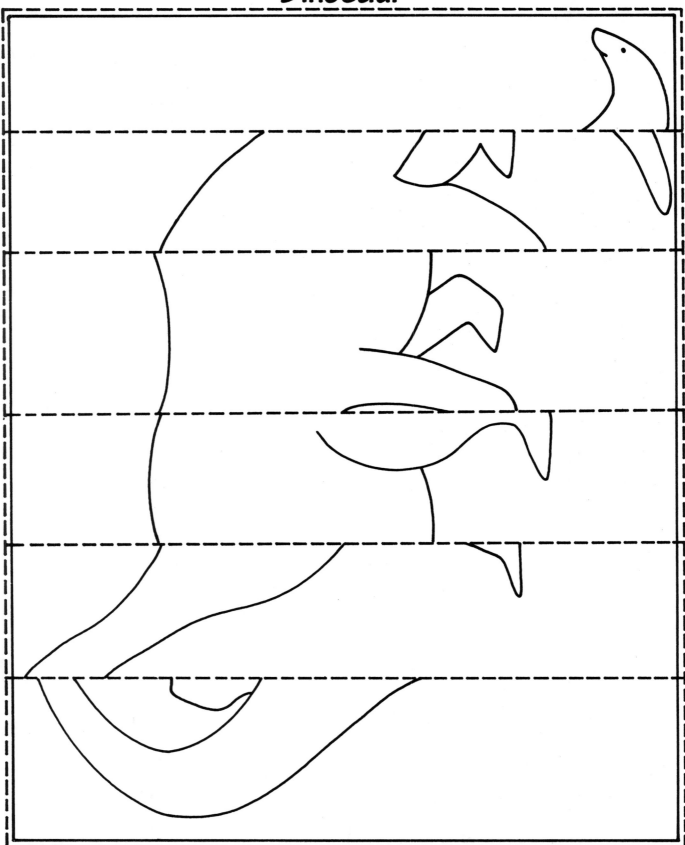

©1995 by Evan-Moor Corp.   186   Readiness Fundamentals

Put the Pieces Together

Pages 188 through 190 require children to create a completed object from separate pieces. This requires that they be able to color and cut out the pieces, then use visual discrimination to put the pieces together to form the correct picture. Have them arrange pieces, then ask the teacher or a partner to verify they are correct before pasting the pieces down. Have children:

1. Color the pieces.
2. Cut out the pieces.
3. Arrange the pieces correctly.
4. Paste the pieces to a large sheet of drawing paper.
5. Add background using crayons.

Teacher: Children need to paste the shapes to a sheet of construction paper.

Make a Wagon

color   Cut   Paste

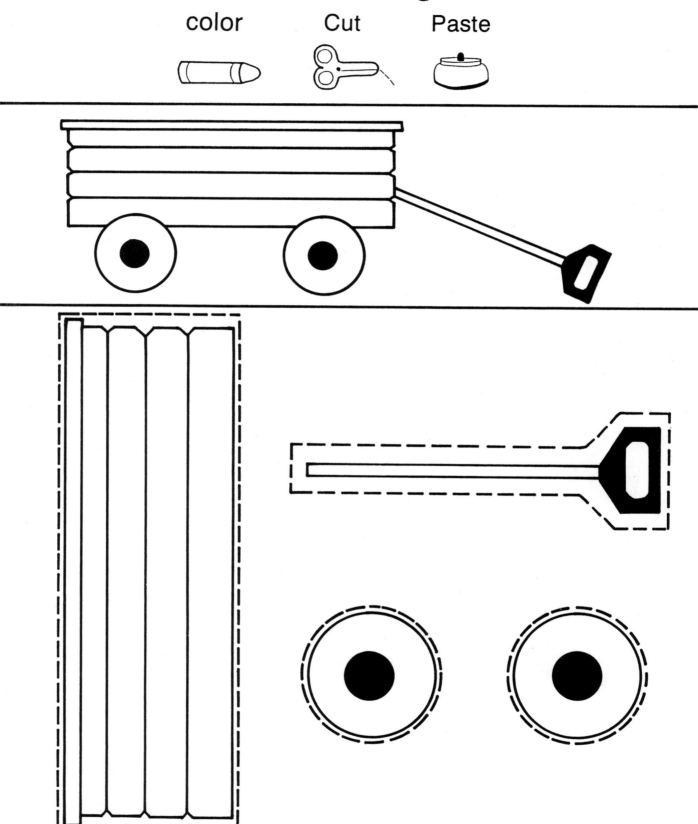

Readiness Fundamentals

Teacher: Children need to paste the shapes to a sheet of construction paper.

Make a Squirrel

189

Readiness Fundamentals

Make a Ship

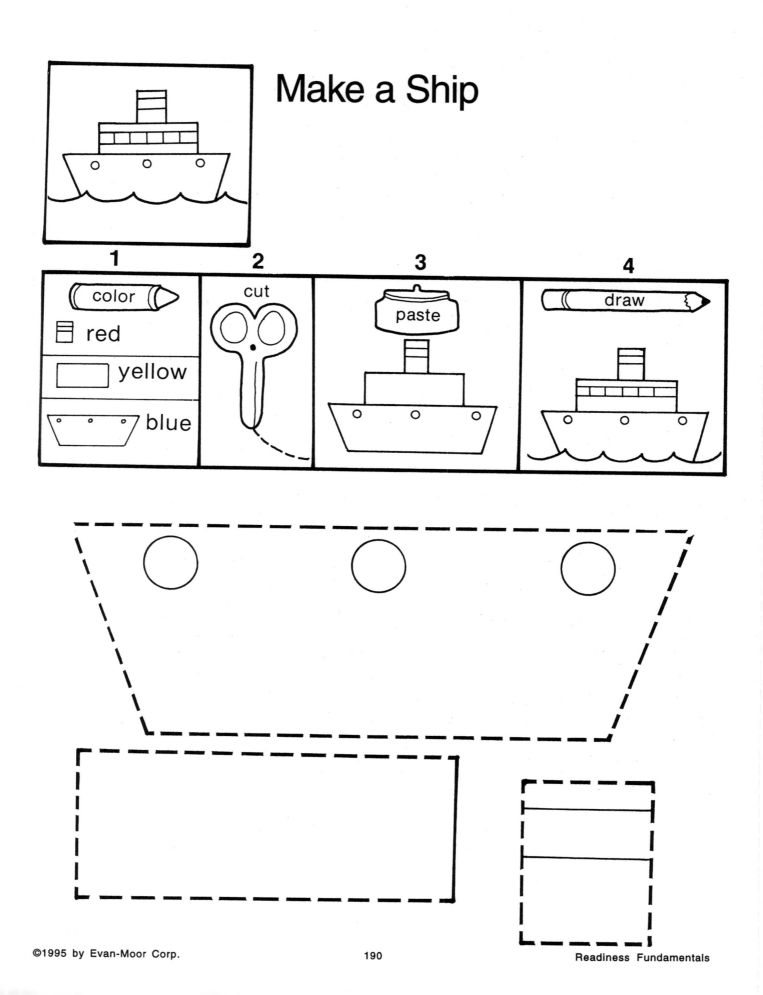

1 color
red
yellow
blue

2 cut

3 paste

4 draw

190

Oral Language Skills

Listening and speaking go hand in hand. The activities described in the section provide practice in both skills.

Conversation is important to learning. You can't have a "silent" classroom and have much learning taking place. Children (and adults) need to talk about what is happening, to share ideas, to ask questions. We need to provide opportunities for this to happen every day.

Through a wide variety of experiences, section five provides opportunities for children to...

- talk with others about personally meaningful experiences
- describe objects, events, and relationships
- have fun with language: rhyming, making up stories
- have one's own language written down and read back
- describe:
    relative positions
    directions and distances
    shapes
    feelings
- explain how
- explore language through dramatic play

Come Together

Opening the Day

The daily routine of starting class provides the first opportunity of the day for getting children to speak.

1. Have someone come up to the calendar and give the day of the week and the full date. Have another child lead the Pledge of Allegiance, and choose a third to lead the opening song (if you have one). These are small activities but provide an opportunity for children to become comfortable speaking in front of a group.

2. Spend a little time remembering what occurred in class yesterday.

3. Take a quick look around the classroom with children explaining what they see in play areas, learning centers, and on the walls (bulletin boards, charts, pictures, etc.).

4. Discuss what will be happening today. Allow children to help plan the day as much as possible.

Closing the Day

End the day by recalling what has taken place today; what they did, what they learned, and what they made. Record this in some way.

S	M	T	W	Th	F	S
		1	2 Joan	3	4	5
6	7	8	9	10	11	12
13	14	15	16	17	18	19
20	21	22	23	24	25	26
27	28	29	30			

Readiness Fundamentals

Sharing

Spontaneous

Children share with their classmates what they have done, are doing, and want to do all through the day as they play and work together. This spontaneous sharing is a great opportunity for the teacher to observe children's language development. Take part in these conversations as you move around the room.

Share and Tell

The traditional methods of sharing times provide changes for a variety of speaking experiences. These may be free choice times where a number of children talk about anything they wish, or may be more structured. Select a specific number of children to share on a given day and assign a topic (the complexity will depend on the age and maturity of your students):

- bring your favorite toy and tell about it
      where it came from
      how you play with it
      why it is your favorite

- bring in a picture of someone in your family
  and tell about that person
      who the person is
      how you are related
      what is special about this person

- come ready to tell about your favorite holiday
      what the holiday is called
      when it is celebrated
      how your family celebrates the holiday

About Me

Have children tell about themselves giving as much information as they are able. Be prepared to guide hesitant children with questions.

"What is your whole name?"

"What is your favorite _____?"

"Do you have a pet? Tell us about it."

"Do you have any bothers and sisters?

Tell us about them?"

Around the Circle

Sit children in a circle and set up opportunities for children to answer in words, phrases, and sentences. This can be very helpful especially for shy children, children with limited backgrounds, and students with limited English since they are allowed to answer with words, phrases, and simple sentences. At the same time they have the opportunity to hear how other students answer.

1. Ask a question which everyone has a turn to answer. Allow "pass" as an option, but keep an eye out for child who always "passes" so you can offer more encouragement to get them to speak. These questions can be as simple as:

What is your name?

How old are you?

What did you eat for breakfast?

They may be more complicated if your students are ready.

Tell us about your _____?

(grandmother, sister, etc.)

What makes you laugh?

Describe your_____.

(birthday party, vacation, etc.) .

2. Pass an object. Ask children to give a word that describes the object. Remind them of the ways you can describe something - color, size, shape, texture, smell, taste, use, etc. In the beginning you will probably get some repetitions, accept these, but work toward helping children move to the point they can each give a different describing word or phrase. For example:

• Pass around a paintbrush.

"How can you use a paintbrush?"

I like to paint pictures of my dog.

Mommy puts my paintings on the refrigerator.

I don't like to paint. It's messy!

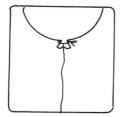

• Pass around a balloon.

"What does this balloon look like?"

It's red.

The balloon is round.

There's a string around the end.

Readiness Fundamentals

It Happened to Me

A child saying *"I got new shoes. Aren't they pretty."* can lead to children talking about their own shoes, trips to the shoe store, the time they lost a shoe, etc. Take advantage of these openings to provide opportunities for children to talk about meaningful experiences in their lives.

These moments may occur spontaneously as in the statements listed above, or my occur as you are reading a book to the class, are working on a skill, come across a picture, have a visitor in class, etc. Share about your own life to model ways in which this can be done.

This sharing can occur in a whole-class setting or in smaller groups of students.

 Readiness Fundamentals

Ask or Tell

Many children, especially young ones, have a great deal of difficulty differentiating between what constitutes a question and an answer. Often, when required to ask a question about a topic, they tell what they already know about it. The following activities help children practice recognizing the difference, then using questions and answers.

Is it a Question or is it an Answer?

1. Prepare two bags using the picture cards below. One bag represents "asking" sentences; the other represents "telling" sentences.
2. Have a group of children sit with you. Place the two bags in front of you with the pictures facing the children. Have several objects available to use for the activity.
3. Model the difference between asking and telling. Show an object such as a blue crayon. Say *"I'm going to tell you something about this. This is a blue crayon."* Then put it into the **"Tell"** bag. Take it out and say. *"Now I'm going to ask you something about this. What color is this crayon?"* Put it into the **"Ask"** bag. Repeat until the children understand that a question (ask) requires an answer, but a statement (tell) doesn't.
4. Let the children try a few times with your help.

I Have a Question. Do You Have an Answer?

Children work in pairs. One child says *"I have a question."*, asks the question, then says *"Do you have an answer?"* The other child says, *"I have an answer."*, replies with the answer, then takes a turn repeating the questioning process.

> Child 1 -*"I have a question. What color is my shirt? Do you have an answer?"*

> Child 2 - *"I have an answer. Your shirt is red."*

Chants, Rhymes, and Poems

Children need to build rich vocabularies and have plenty of concepts to draw on if they are going to be able to speak in a clear and interesting manner. There are many ways to help children reach this goal. You can begin at the readiness level with chants, poems, and refrains. The rhythm and rhyme helps children recall the words and the ideas being taught. It also provides shy children or those with limited language to participate orally in a successful manner.

Select rhymes, chants, and refrains from:
- Nursery Rhymes
  "Humpty Dumpty
  Sat on the wall..."
- Refrains in Stories
  "He huffed and he puffed and
  he blew the house down."
- Jumprope and Game Rhymes
  "Teddy Bear, Teddy Bear
  Turn around..."
- Poems about Subjects
  Math - "1, 2, 3, 4,
       Dragons are knocking at my door"
       "One, Two, Buckle my shoe..."
       "Five furry kittens..."
  Science - "Octopus"
       "Spider"
       "Hamster"

Pages 198 to 205 contain examples of chants and rhymes you might use with your children. You can give copies of the pages to your students to color and take home after they have learned the chant or refrain.

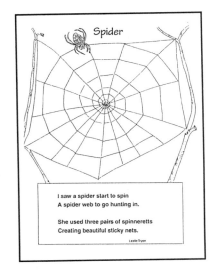

Spider

I saw a spider start to spin
A spider web to go hunting in.

She used three pairs of spinneretts
Creating beautiful sticky nets.

Leslie Tryon

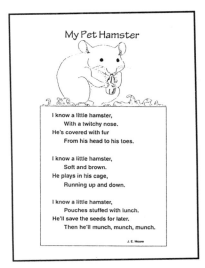

My Pet Hamster

I know a little hamster,
   With a twitchy nose.
He's covered with fur
   From his head to his toes.

I know a little hamster,
   Soft and brown.
He plays in his cage,
   Running up and down.

I know a little hamster,
   Pouches stuffed with lunch.
He'll save the seeds for later.
   Then he'll munch, munch, munch.

J. E. Moore

Note: Act out the motions as you recite the verse.

Teddy Bear

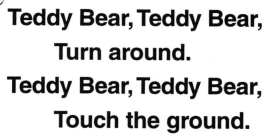

Teddy Bear, Teddy Bear,
Turn around.
Teddy Bear, Teddy Bear,
Touch the ground.

Teddy Bear, Teddy Bear,
Read the news.
Teddy Bear, Teddy Bear,
Shine your shoes

Teddy Bear, Teddy Bear,
Go upstairs.
Teddy Bear, Teddy Bear,
Say your prayers.

Teddy Bear, Teddy Bear,
Turn out the light.
Teddy Bear, Teddy Bear,
Say "Goodnight."

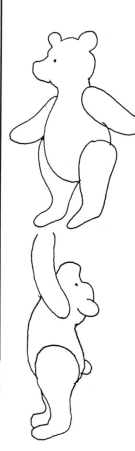

Dragons at the Door

1, 2, 3, 4
Dragons are knocking at my door.

5, 6, 7, 8
It sounds like they can hardly wait.

9 knocks, then 10
Shall I go and let them in?

Readiness Fundamentals

One, Two,
Buckle My Shoe

1
2

One, two,
Buckle my shoe.

3
4

Three, four,
Shut the door.

5
6

Five, six,
Pick up sticks.

7
8

Seven, eight,
Lay them straight.

9
10

Nine, ten,
Start again.

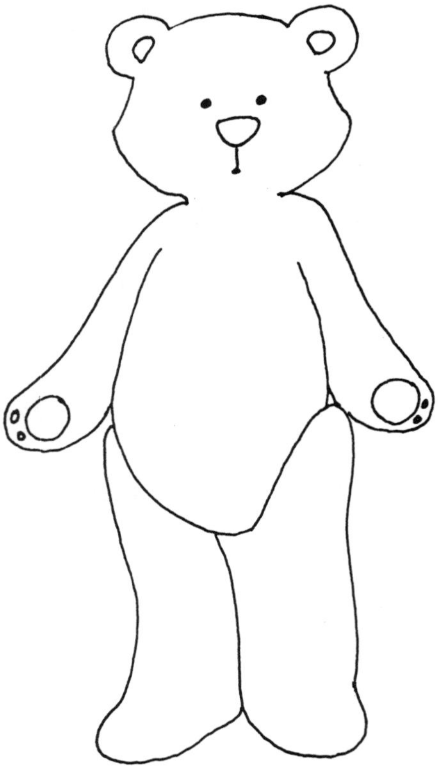

Five Furry Kittens

Five furry kittens one spring night
Sat on a fence. What a funny sight!

The first one danced on his kitty toes.
The second one washed his little black nose.
The third one turned around and around.
The fourth one jumped down to the ground.
The fifth one sang a kitty song.

Five furry kittens played all night long.

J.E. Moore

Note: Review the facts about an octopus after you recite the verse.

Octopus

One leg

Two legs

Three legs

Four!

You mean to say

that you have more?

Five legs

Six legs

Seven legs

Eight!

An octopus is really great!

Leslie Tryon

 Readiness Fundamentals

Spider

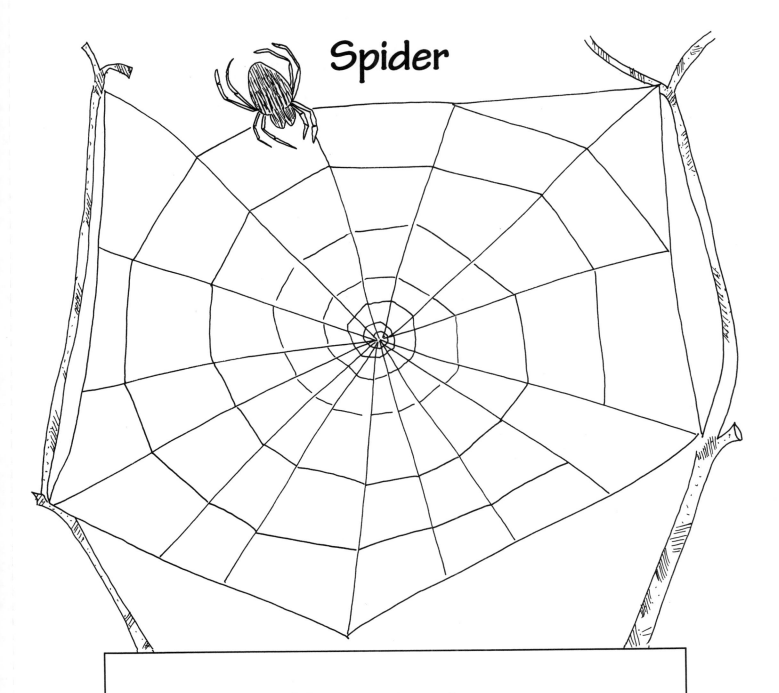

I saw a spider start to spin
A spider web to go hunting in.

She used three pairs of spinneretts
Creating beautiful sticky nets.

Leslie Tryon

Readiness Fundamentals

My Pet Hamster

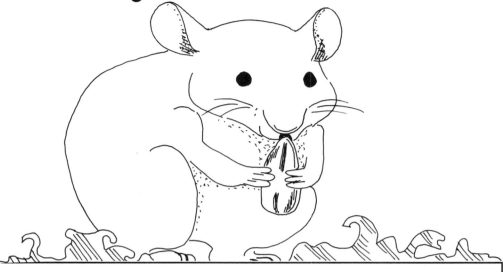

I know a little hamster,
> With a twitchy nose.

He's covered with fur
> From his head to his toes.

I know a little hamster,
> Soft and brown.

He plays in his cage,
> Running up and down.

I know a little hamster,
> Pouches stuffed with lunch.

He'll save the seeds for later.
> Then he'll munch, munch, munch.

J. E. Moore

Readiness Fundamentals

Hatch a Chick

Come out, little chick.

Come out, little chick.

Pick at your shell.

That's the trick.

I'll try to be quick.

But this shell is so thick.

Pick.

Pick.

Pick.

Come out, little chick.

Come out, little chick.

Pick at your shell.

That's the trick.

Leslie Tryon

Readiness Fundamentals

Tell a Story

★Children are great at telling stories to themselves and friends as they are playing imaginative games. Take advantage of this interest in stories to help develop speaking skills. Start by telling stories to your students. These stories can be from literature, from your own life, or from your imagination. Children love to be <u>told</u> stories. You can help them learn to love to <u>tell</u> stories. Don't expect miracles in the beginning. This is an on-going process and some children will progress more slowly than others.

1. Read or tell a story to your students.
   Ask them to recall events from the story you told.
   > *"Red Riding Hood went into the bears' house."*
   > *"She ate the porridge."*

2. Ask children to retell a familiar story (folktales work well for this).
   > *"There were three goats. One goat went over the bridge.*
   > *The gross ugly troll said 'Who's walking over my bridge'...."*

3. Start a simple story. Ask children to tell what happened next.
   > *"Jai and Lee went to the park. They found a ball..."*
   > *"Stacy caught the measles. She had to...."*

4. Have children tell a story from their own family.
   > *"When my grandpa was little he let the chickens get out of the*
   > *pen. His daddy was real mad. He had to sit in the corner and*
   > *didn't get to eat his dinner."*

5. Show a picture and ask children to tell a short story about the picture.
   > *"There is a boy on a bike. He is going up the hill to play*
   > *with his friend." The boy on the bike is going to the store to*
   > *get milk for his mama."*

6. Have children draw or paint a picture that tells a story, then share it with the class.
   > *"This is my cat Bob. He is sitting by the window looking at the bird.*
   > *He wants to get out so he can catch the bird. He is a good hunter."*

★Use the picture cards on pages 207-209 to stimulate the retelling of familiar stories with your students.

Readiness Fundamentals

Readiness Fundamentals

Describing Things
By Characteristics

Words that Describe
Review words that describe. Show a series of objects.
Ask children to describe by a given characteristic.

- color - lay out a row of colored blocks
- size - show balls in various sizes
- shape - lay out a collection of attribute blocks
- smell - put out cotton balls soaked in different smells
- material/texture - have objects made from various materials to use for describing by texture and by the material an object was made from

Basket of Objects
Fill a basket with objects. These may be miscellaneous objects picked up around the classroom or may have a "theme" (school tools, gardening implements, clothing types, etc.). Go over the items with students to be sure they can name the objects and know how they are used.

Model the process to be followed. "This is a pencil. It is long and thin. It is yellow. It is made of wood and graphite. I use it to write letters and draw pictures."
"This is an egg beater. It is made of metal. It has parts that turn. I use it to beat up eggs before I cook them."

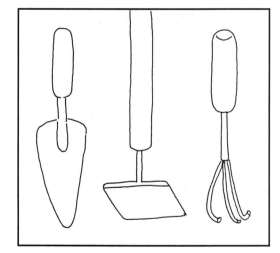

Have each child doing the activity pick out one object and describe it. Be ready to ask helpful questions if the child has difficulty.

Pick a Picture
Put a series of pictures (see pages 212-215) out for children to see. Ask a child to take a card and describe it to the rest of the group. This can be done as a simple describing lesson, or children can select one of the pictures in their mind, describe it aloud, and have classmates try to pick the card being described.

           Readiness Fundamentals

What's in My Bag?

How to Make

1. You'll need one lunch-sized paper bag per player and some objects found in the classroom (for example: crayons, toys, blocks, apple, ball, etc.).

2. Put one item in each bag and fold the top closed.

How to Play

Children sit in a line facing the teacher. The teacher has the bags.

A child picks a bag and stands by the teacher. He/She peeks inside the ag and them gives a description of the object, ending by asking, ***"What's in my bag?"***

The other children try to guess what is in the bag. The game ends when each child has had a turn to describe what is in the bag.

Helpful Hints

This game is not as easy for children as it sounds. Be prepared to prompt the child doing the describing. Ask questions such as:

"What color is it?"
"What is it used for?"
"What is it made of?"
"Can you eat it?"
"What shape is it?"
"How big is it?"

The picture cards on the following pages can be used in the paper bags also.

Note: Reproduce these cards to use the activities on pages 210 and 211.

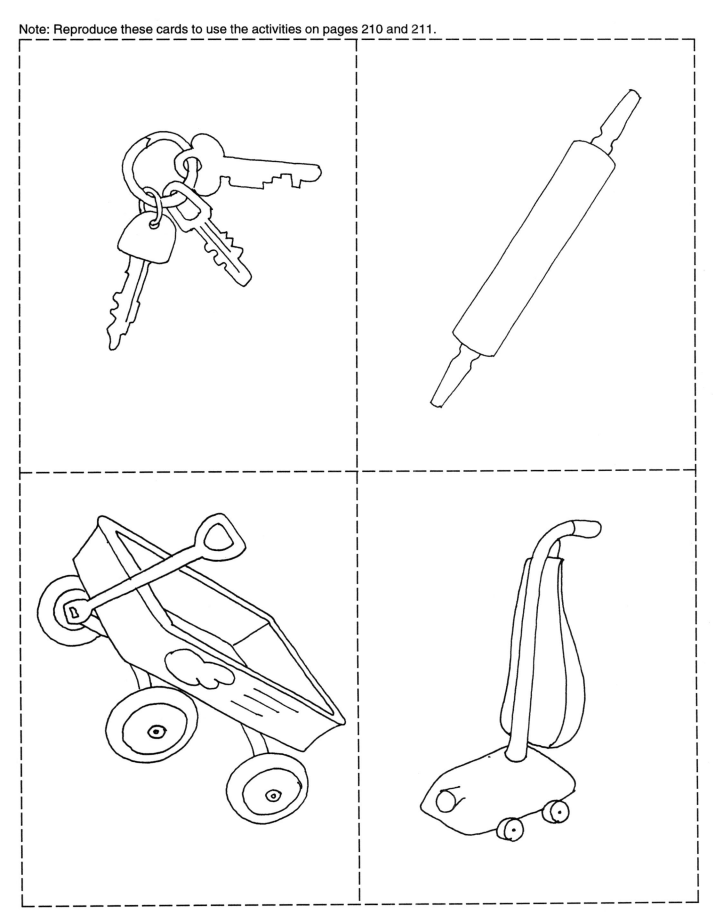

Readiness Fundamentals

Note: Reproduce these cards to use the activities on pages 210 and 211.

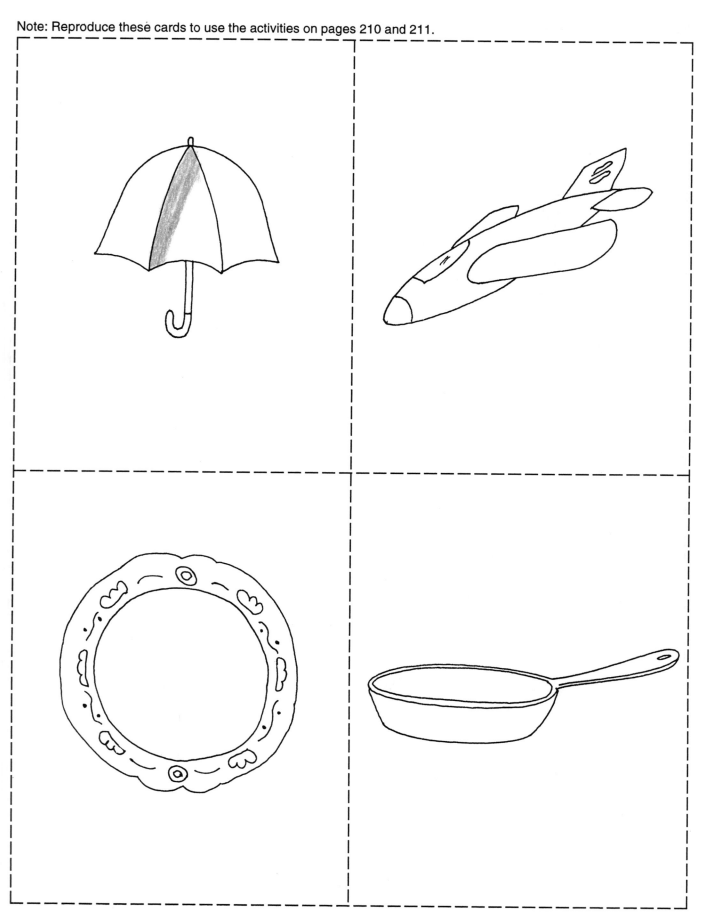

Note: Reproduce these cards to use the activities on pages 210 and 211.

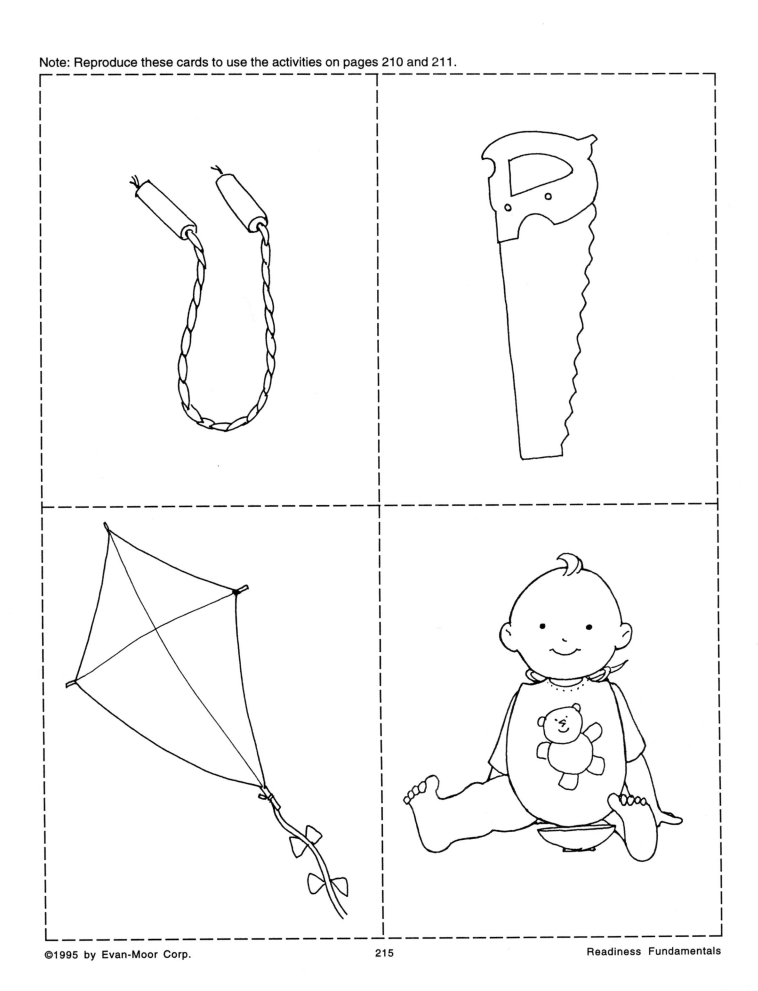

Describing Things
Positional Words

Review words that describe where things are located.
Model each activity before you ask children to do it.

Where are You?

Have children sit in various places around the room, then
tell where they are.

"*I am sitting on a chair.*"

"*I am behind the table.*"

"*I am under the table.*"

"*I am next to the desk.*"

"*I am in front of the door.*"

I Put it...?

A child chooses a stuffed animal and places it in
somewhere, then tells class where it located using positional
words.

"*I put (bear)   (under the table) .*"

"*I put (the mouse) (on top of the big book) .*"

"*The   (big dog) is (behind the teacher) .*"

"*The   (toy) is (in the waste basket) .*"

"*My   (dolly) is (beside me on the chair) .*"

Paint and Tell

Have children paint a picture with at least two items in it.
They share the pictures with the group, telling where the
objects are located.

"*My blue kite is flying up in the sky.*"

"*The little bunny is by a big tree.*"

"*These flowers are growing next to the house.*"

"*The girl's trike is on the sidewalk.*"

"*The grandmother is by the stove making cookies.*"

Readiness Fundamentals

Where's the Bear
One More Time

Use the same bear stick puppets the children make for the activity on page 101-102. If children have already taken these home, make a set of six and have children work with you in small groups.

Hold the bear in various positions and have a student tell where the bear is located. The bear may be place around your own body or in various places around the room. Encourage children to use different words each time. For example:

- Place the bear behind your knee and ask *"Where the bear?"*
Child replies *"The bear is behind your knee."*

- Place the bear inside a book shelf and ask *"Where's the bear?"*
Child answers *"The bear is inside the book shelf."*

- Place the bear beneath a chair and ask *"Where's the bear/"*
Child says *"The bear puppet is hiding under the chair."*

Have children hold their bear puppets somewhere and tell the location:

"My bear is over my head."

"My bear is in my desk."

"My bear is on Tommie's table."

Little Boy Blue

Where are Little Boy Blue, the cows, and the sheep?
Reproduce the form on page 219. Teach the verse:

Little Boy Blue
Come blow your horn.
The sheep's in the meadow.
The cow's in the corn.

Where is the little boy
who looks after the sheep?
He's under the haystack
Fast asleep.

Have children cut out their pieces. Have them lay the pieces (don't glue yet) on the picture sheet according to your oral directions. Give them **wrong** directions on where to put each picture. See if they can correctly rearrange the pictures into the correct places.

Have them paste the pictures in place when they have made the corrections.

Finally, have everyone recite the verse again, touching the pictures as they are named.

Little Boy Blue

paste

paste

paste

Readiness Fundamentals

Rosie's Walk

Read **Rosie's Walk** by Pat Hutchins to your class.
Discuss all of the places Rosie went on her walk
and locate the fox in each picture in the story.

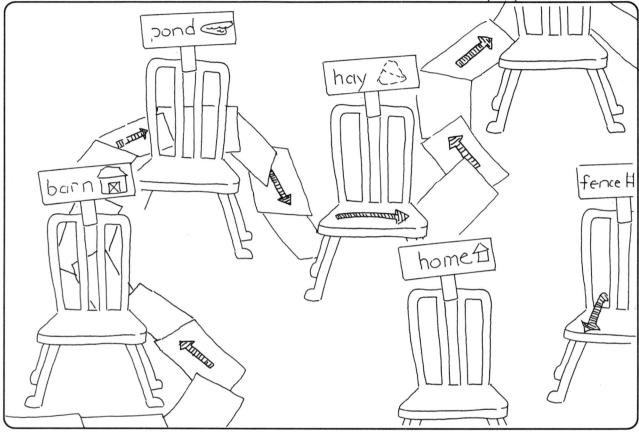

Move Through the Story

Set up a "path" around the classroom to represent the places Rosie walked. Make
the masks on pages 221 and 222. Select a hen and a fox to walk the path as you re-
read the story. Stop at each point and select a child to tell where Rosie is and where
the fox is hiding at that point in the story.

Sequence and Retell

Sequence the story, using the pictures (see pages 223 and 224) for students to retell
the story in their own words. Reproduce the pictures. Cut them apart. Put a Velcro
dot on the back of each picture (to use on a flannel board) or paste them to tag and
laminate to sit on the chalk tray.

Pass out the pictures. Select a child to come up and place his/her picture on the
flannel board. Each subsequent child places his/her picture in the correct place to
sequence the story.

When the pictures are in order, give children a chance to retell the story in their own
words.

Hen Mask

1. Reproduce this pattern on heavy stock.
2. Color and cut it out.
3. Tape a tongue depressor on the back for a handle.

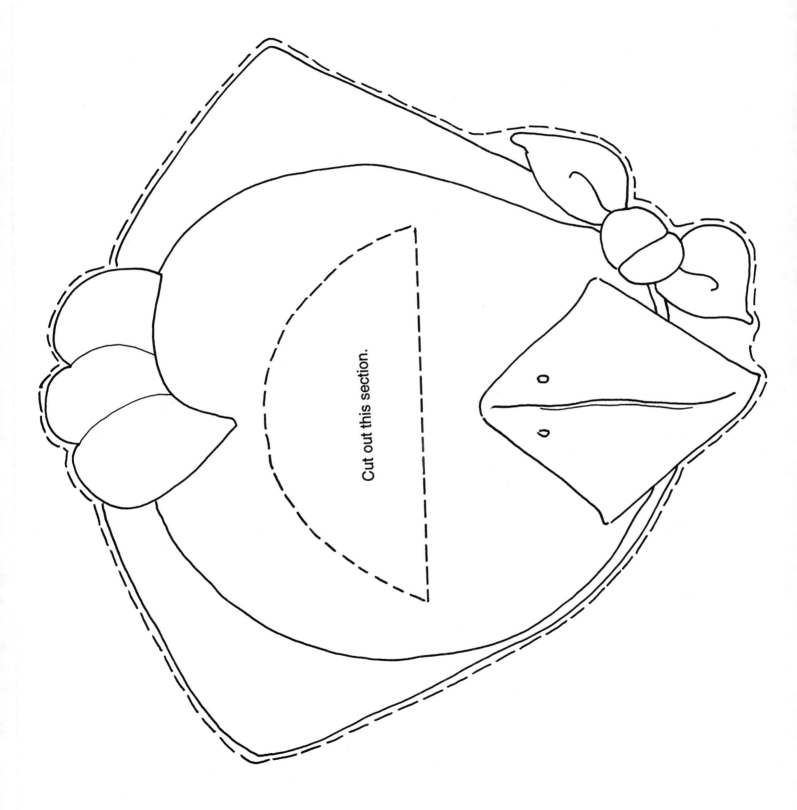

Cut out this section.

Readiness Fundamentals

Fox Mask

1. Reproduce this pattern on heavy stock.
2. Color and cut it out.
3. Tape a tongue depressor on the back for a handle.

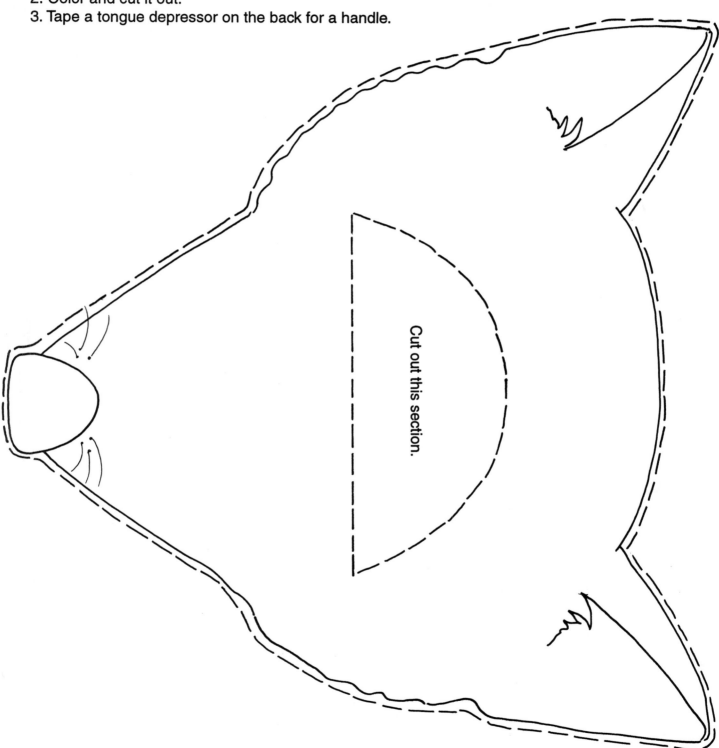

Cut out this section.

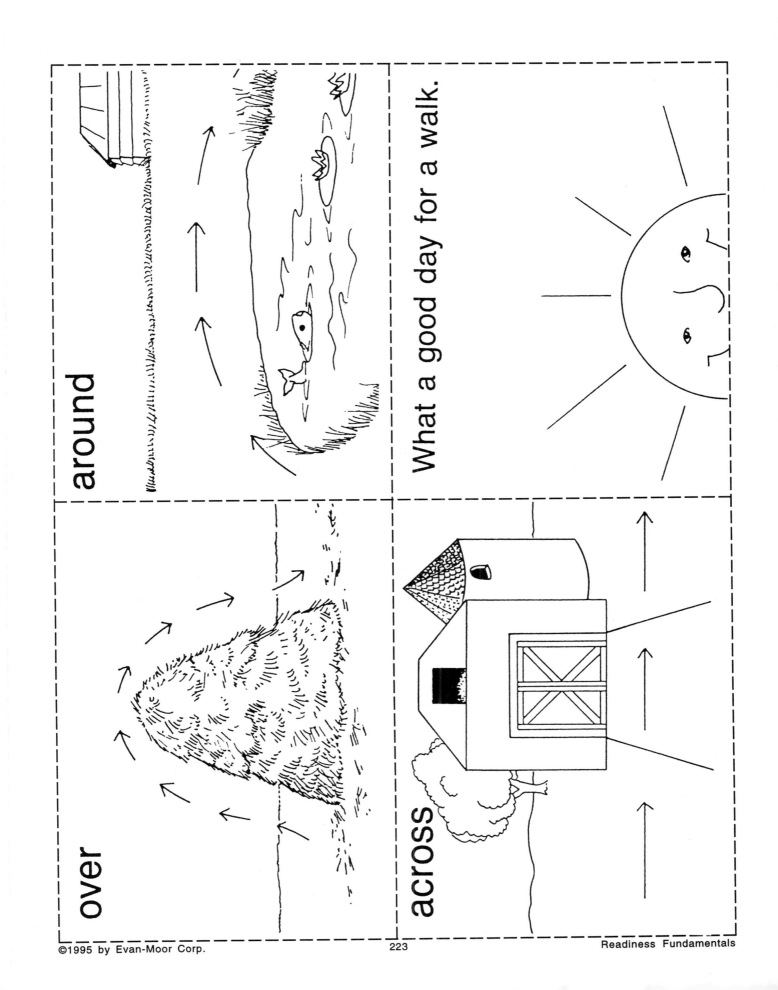

around

What a good day for a walk.

over

across

223

past

under

through

home

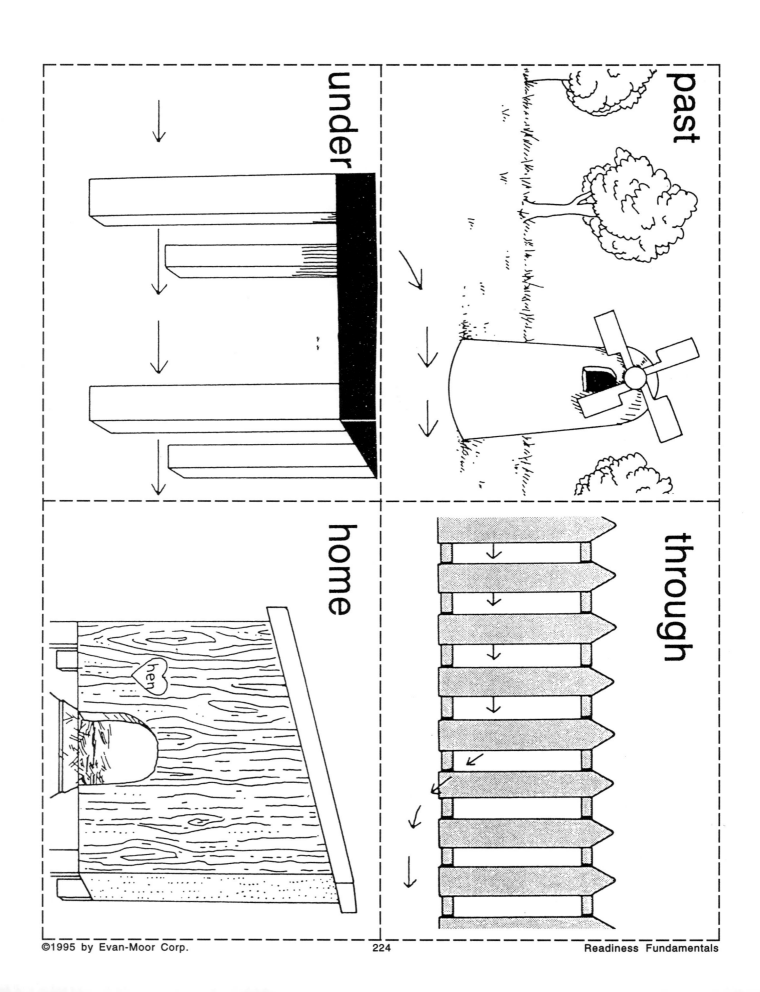

Readiness Fundamentals

Dramatic Play

Dramatic play provides a wonderful opportunity for children to use spoken language.

1. These experiences can take place informally in center play - kitchen center, block center, dress-up center, etc. - where children take on roles as they play.

2. Children can review rhymes, poems, and simple stories using finger puppets or stick puppets. Both forms of puppet can also be used for reporting on factual information children have learned.

See pages 226 and 227 for nursery rhyme finger puppets for: **Humpty Dumpty, Wee Willie Winkie, Jack Jumped Over the Candlestick, Little Miss Muffet.**

See pages 228 and 229 for stick puppet patterns to use to share what has been learned about pets and about farm animal families.

3. Children can act out events from their own lives - visit to the dentist, how to check out a book from the library, helping take care of a pet, meeting a new friend, etc.

4. Children act out what they know about different occupations, people, animals, etc. using masks. Some examples are provided for you on the pages 230 through 237.

5. They can act out favorite stories using simple costumes and props found around the classroom or using headbands and masks.
See pages 238 through 240 for direction on how to set up the room and patterns for a set of headbands to use in acting out **Goldilocks and the Three Bears.**

Note: Students color and cut out the puppets. They make a ring out of the strips of paper and paste the nursery rhyme character to the ring. They wear the finger puppets as they recite the rhyme.

Mother Goose Finger Puppets

Humpty Dumpty

Humpty Dumpty sat on a wall.
Humpty Dumpty had a great fall.
All the King's horses and all the King's men,
Couldn't put Humpty back together again.

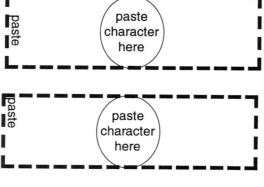

paste

paste character here

paste

paste character here

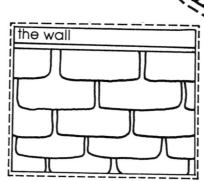

the wall

Wee Willie Winkie

Wee Willie Winkie runs through the town,
Upstairs and downstairs in his nightgown;
Rapping at the window, crying through the lock,
"Are the children in their beds?
Now it's eight o'clock."

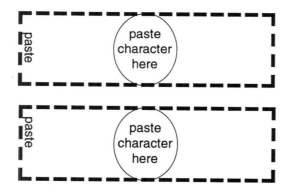

paste

paste character here

paste

paste character here

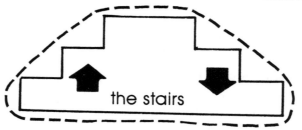

the stairs

Note: Students color and cut out the puppets. They make a ring out of the strips of paper and paste the nursery rhyme character to the ring. They wear the finger puppets as they recite the rhyme.

Mother Goose Finger Puppets

Jack Be Nimble

Jack be nimble, Jack be quick.
Jack jumped over the candlestick.

paste

paste character here

paste

paste character here

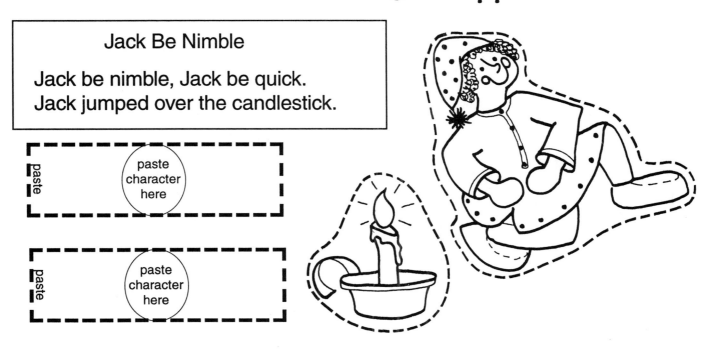

Little Miss Muffet

Little Miss Muffet
Sat on her tuffet,
Eating her curds and whey.
Along came a spider,
And sat down beside her
And frightened Miss Muffet away

paste

paste character here

paste

paste character here

Note: Reproduce these stick puppets for students to report on pets.

Pet Puppet Patterns

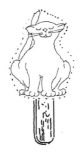

Note: Reproduce these stick puppets for students to report on farm animal families.

Farm Animal Puppet Patterns

Dog Mask

1. Reproduce this pattern on heavy stock.
2. Color and cut it out.
3. Tape a tongue depressor on the back for a handle.

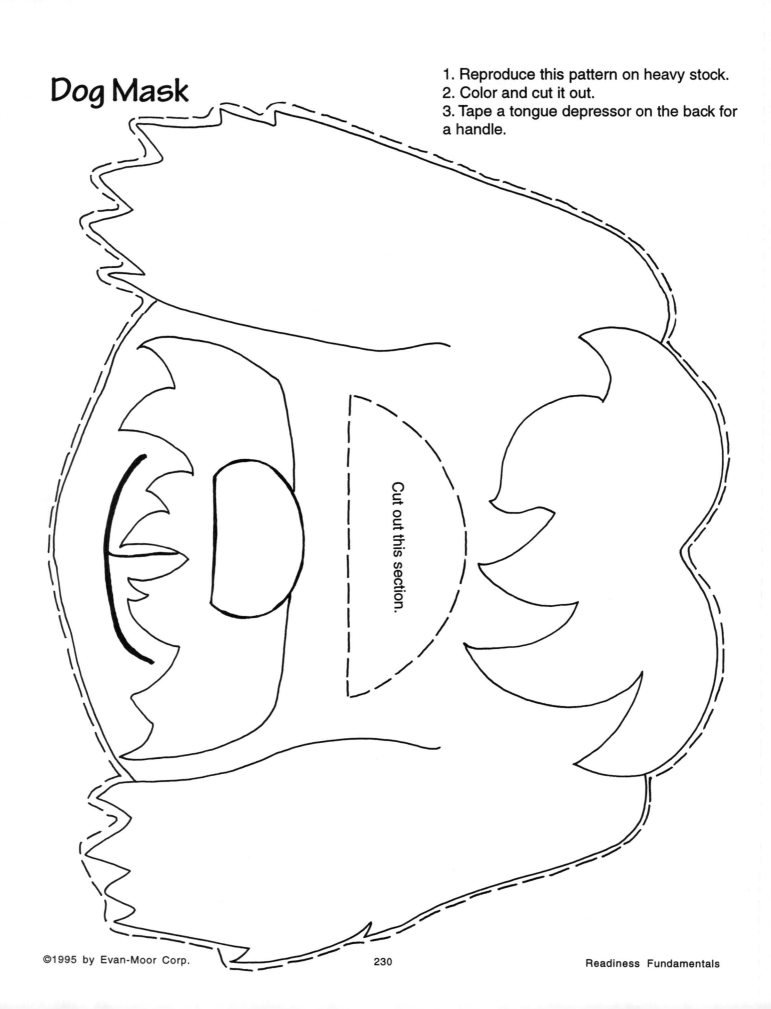

Cut out this section.

Readiness Fundamentals

Monkey Mask

1. Reproduce this pattern on heavy stock.
2. Color and cut it out.
3. Tape a tongue depressor on the back for a handle.

Cut out this section.

Readiness Fundamentals

Lion Mask

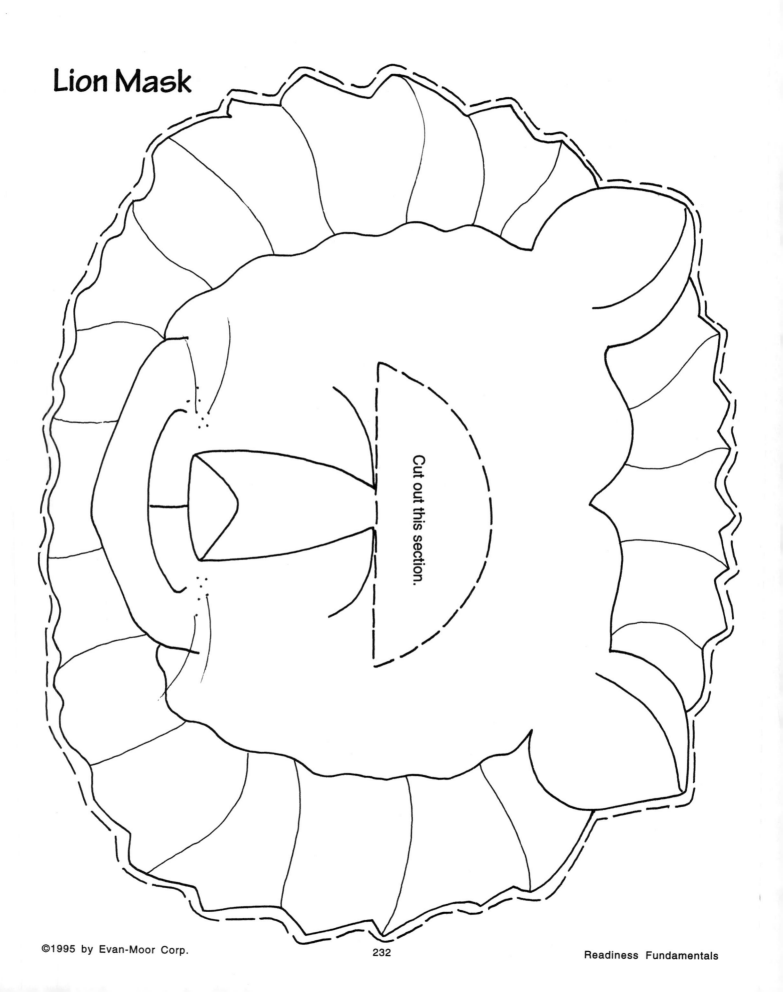

Cut out this section.

Readiness Fundamentals

Police Officer
Mask

1. Reproduce this pattern on heavy stock.
2. Color and cut it out.
3. Tape a tongue depressor on the back for a handle.

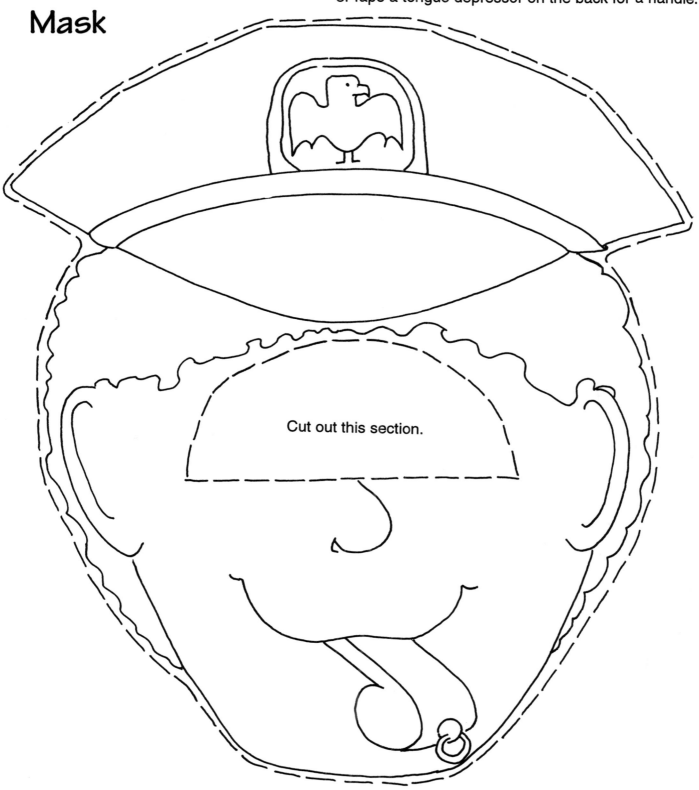

Cut out this section.

Fire Fighter Mask

1. Reproduce this pattern on heavy stock.
2. Color and cut it out.
3. Tape a tongue depressor on the back for a handle.

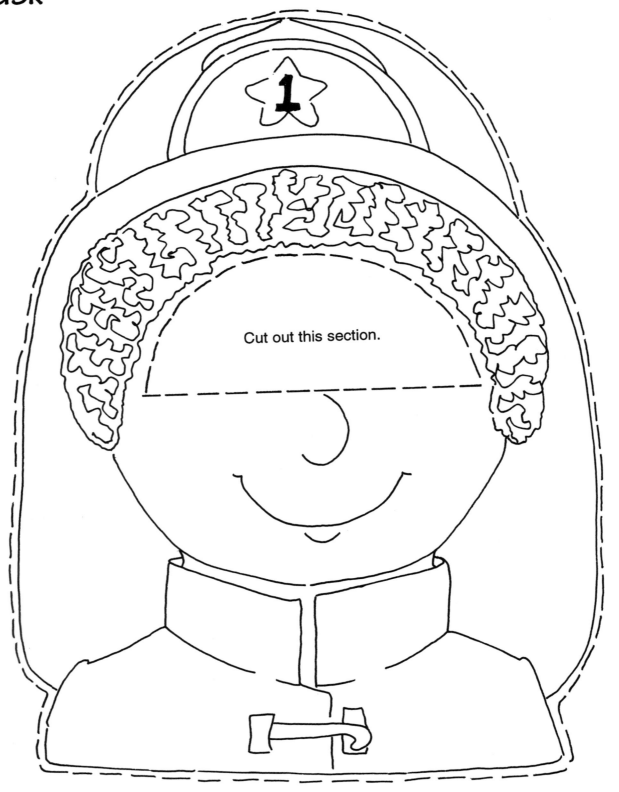

Cut out this section.

Readiness Fundamentals

Doctor Mask

1. Reproduce this pattern on heavy stock.
2. Color and cut it out.
3. Tape a tongue depressor on the back for a handle.

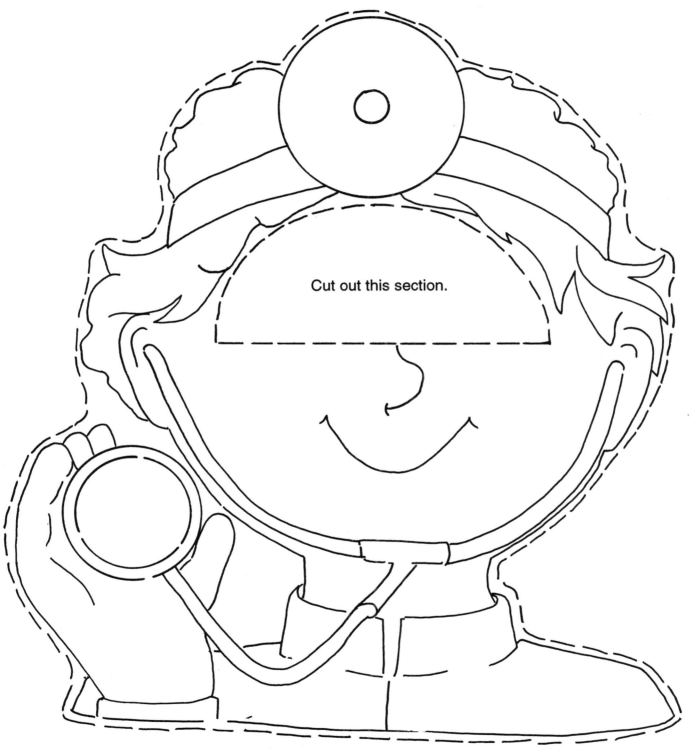

Cut out this section.

Readiness Fundamentals

Robot Mask

1. Reproduce this pattern on heavy stock.
2. Color and cut it out.
3. Tape a tongue depressor on the back for a handle.

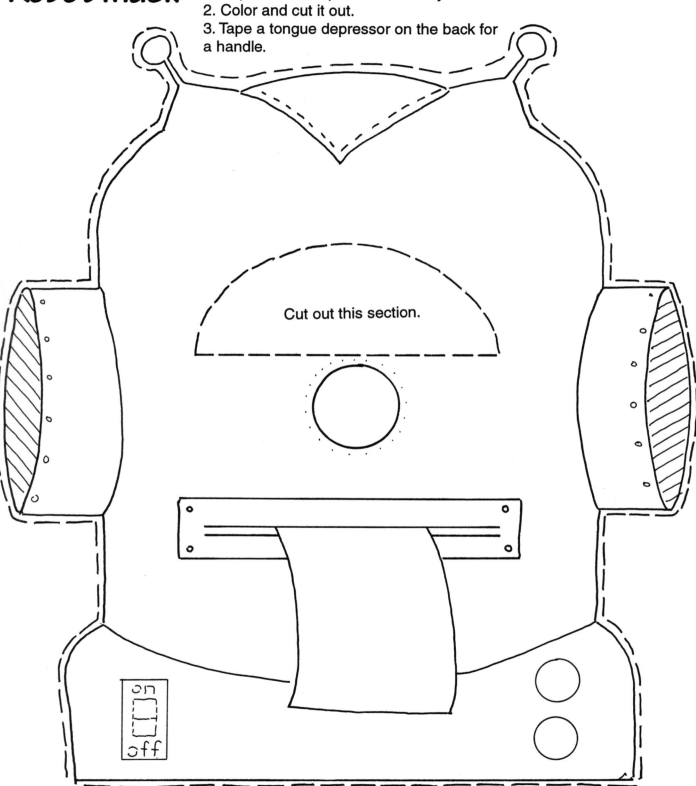

Cut out this section.

on

Clown Mask

1. Reproduce this pattern on heavy stock.
2. Color and cut it out.
3. Tape a tongue depressor on the back for a handle.

Cut out this section.

Presenting
Goldilocks and the Three Bears

Room Setup

The children not having acting parts sit in a circle to form the "walls" of the house. A space is left for the doorway, and two children stand, holding hands, to form the window through which Goldilocks escapes. Line up a table with three bowls, three chairs, and three beds (mats, rugs, or towels on the floor). Then let the action begin. Reproduce the headbands on pages 239 and 240 for students to use to act out the story of Goldilocks and the Three Bears. Encourage the "actors" to use their own words to tell their parts.

How to Make Headbands

1. Reproduce the bear mask three times and make one copy of the Goldilocks mask.

2. Color and cut out the headband parts.

3. Cut two strips of construction paper (2 1/2" x 11" or 6.5 X 28 cm).

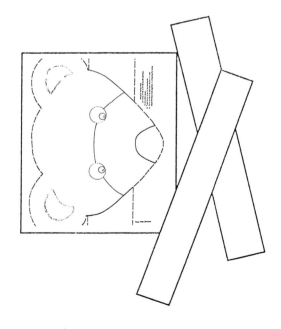

4. Paste the construction paper stirps to the sides of the headband pattern.

4. Fit the headband on the student's head. Overlap the paper strips to a comfortable spot and staple the ends in place.

Goldilocks

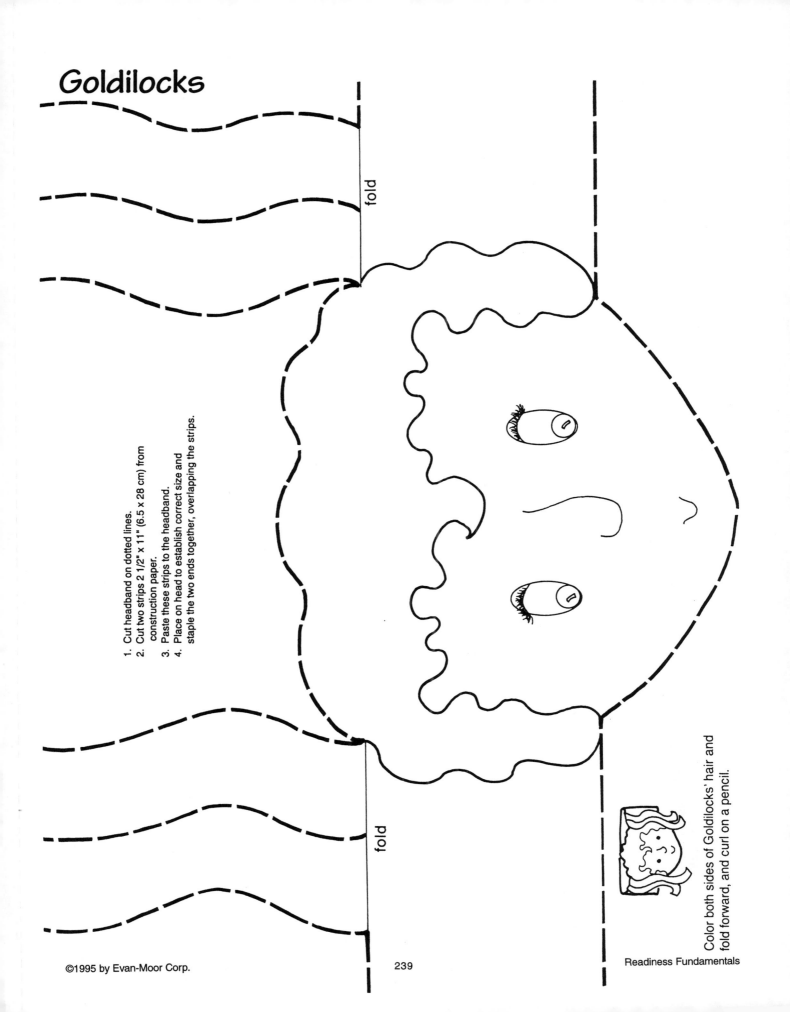

fold

fold

1. Cut headband on dotted lines.
2. Cut two strips 2 1/2" x 11" (6.5 x 28 cm) from construction paper.
3. Paste these strips to the headband.
4. Place on head to establish correct size and staple the two ends together, overlapping the strips.

Color both sides of Goldilocks' hair and fold forward, and curl on a pencil.

Readiness Fundamentals

Bear
Headband

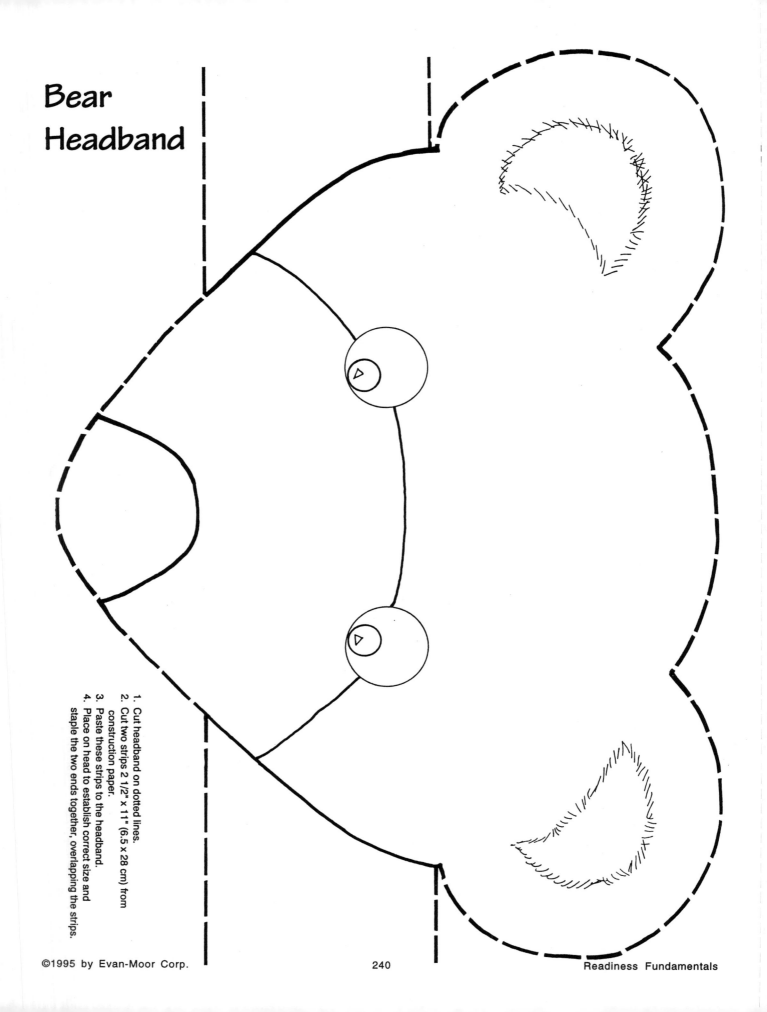

1. Cut headband on dotted lines.
2. Cut two strips 2 1/2" x 11" (6.5 x 28 cm) from construction paper.
3. Paste these strips to the headband.
4. Place on head to establish correct size and staple the two ends together, overlapping the strips.

Readiness Fundamentals